◆ FriesenPress

One Printers Way
Altona, MB R0G 0B0
Canada

www.friesenpress.com

Copyright © 2023 by James R. Schmalenberg
First Edition — 2023

All rights reserved.

No part of this publication may be reproduced in any form, or by any means, electronic or mechanical, including photocopying, recording, or any information browsing, storage, or retrieval system, without permission in writing from FriesenPress.

ISBN
978-1-03-917090-2 (Hardcover)
978-1-03-917089-6 (Paperback)
978-1-03-917091-9 (eBook)

1. SELF-HELP, PERSONAL GROWTH, SUCCESS

Distributed to the trade by The Ingram Book Company

Life Really Isn't All That Complicated

But You Do Have To Think

by James R. Schmalenberg

1. Finding Your Genius

"We all have genius within us, never doubt that fact."
— CATHERINE PULSIFER

Life as a Free-Range Chicken

I can almost hear most of you thinking, "What do free-range chickens have to do with finding your genius?" Well, in fact, a great deal, but first you need some background on my upbringing as the free-range chicken's friend.

I grew up in a small prairie town in the 1950s and 1960s. Life really was simpler then. Our parents, for the most part, were good parents, but they certainly were not the helicopter parents hovering over their children that we see today. Children—especially during the spring, summer, and fall—spent most of their non-school time playing with little or no supervision. In the 1950s, we had no TV, no smart phones, no computers, and certainly no internet. We played outside most of the day. Our time outside included playing pick-up games of most sports and hide-and-seek, climbing trees, and generally enjoying being outside. We even had our own swimming hole aptly named "bare bum beach."

As an example of how much simpler life was, I can remember when I was about six, getting up very early one fall day before anyone in the house was up, and going down to the local skating rink, which had been converted to a barn for the livestock in the local agricultural fair.

Farmers from the area brought their cows, pigs, chickens, and other livestock to the fair to be judged. This was a fascinating time for a six-year-old, and as I recall, neither of my parents seemed to think that it was a problem that I left for a few hours on my own. As I said, life really was simpler then.

Now, back to the free-range chicken story. My life was fairly unstructured, but I still had basic parental rules. My friend Sam, however, lived a very unstructured life, and he, to this day, describes his upbringing as similar to a free-range chicken. He would get up in the morning, dress himself, and spend most of the non-school days wondering around town. Mothers and fathers in town soon realized that Sam had very little home support, and as a result, they would feed him, clean him up a little, and send him on his way, or if, for example, Sam's team had a hockey game that day, they would give him a ride to the game and ensure that he had all his equipment. Birthday parties were a highlight for Sam since, whether invited to the party or not, he was usually invited in for hotdogs and cake. Sam really was the town's free-range chicken.

I'm sure that you are wondering how Sam turned out. In fact, he turned out great. As a free-range chicken, Sam learned that most people are good, that they will help you when you need a hand, and they expect nothing in return. Sam became this type of person himself. I am convinced that Sam's genius was his people skills and his belief in the innate goodness of people. I am convinced that he developed this skill as a result of his free-range chicken upbringing. If he was going to eat regularly and take part in all the activities that the other kids did, he needed to depend on the goodness of a great many people.

The key point that I am making is that most of us don't have a "free-range chicken" type of upbringing, but we all, out of necessity, must find our way in the world and determine what our genius is and, in addition, gain an understanding of a number of other basic life building blocks. This is much more challenging to do than most of us realize when we start life's journey. We simply don't know what we don't know. For example, how many eighteen-year-olds understand the importance of:

1. Finding Your Genius

- Developing excellent people skills, including the ability to sell?
- Financial knowledge?
- Setting and achieving goals?

These skills were not taught in any classroom I was ever in, or even mentioned in passing, and my parents certainly didn't coach me in these skills. For the most part, if we learned any of these skills, it was by following the example set by family and friends.

What's Your Free-Range Chicken Skill?

Most of us spend a great deal of our life trying to figure out what we are good at and what our role is in this life. On top of that, we are told that we must overcome our weaknesses so that we can become a well-rounded person. I believe that this is absolutely wrong! I am convinced that our weaknesses only need be overcome if they seriously impede our strengths. We all have strengths, and most of us have one or two in which we truly excel—these are our genius skills.

I believe that the correct path is to find your true genius and focus your energy on developing this skill while supplementing this with the basic life skills that we can all use, such as developing positive habits, financial management, and setting and achieving your goals. The rest of this book focuses on these fundamental skills and basic knowledge that I certainly didn't have until later in life.

If I have a genius, it's that I see things a little differently than most people—I try to break concepts down into their basic components so that I see the big picture, and if need be, I can work with the details as required. For example, I remember the first, and only, accounting class that I took in university. The first few weeks seemed to be nothing but mind-numbing detail, and I really hated that class, but then I started to see the big picture and the basic accounting principles:

1. In double-entry accounting, the debits and credits must be equal. If you debit one account, you had better credit another account or you won't balance. Accountants are as anal as I am and insist that you balance.

2. The balance sheet is one of the fundamental statements, and in the balance sheet, assets minus liabilities equals net worth. The balance sheet tells you at a point in time how much you are worth—nice for individuals and businesses to know. For example, if you only have one major asset, like your house, which is worth $500,000 with a liability of a mortgage of $300,000, then you have a net worth of $200,000. This is a gross simplification, of course, as most people have many more assets and liabilities.

3. The income statement is a second fundamental accounting statement. This statement uses the basic principle that revenue minus expenses over a period of time tells you your profit or loss for that accounting period. Again, very useful for both individuals and businesses.

Now, I am sure that any accountant reading this will tell you that there is a great deal more to accounting than I have outlined above, but knowing these three concepts and thinking through the accounting problems that I faced in Accounting 101, got me an A—and believe me, I did not enjoy accounting. Unfortunately, many professional educators get into the details without thoroughly explaining the basic concepts first. The metaphor that my father often used was that people often can't see the forest for the trees. In other words, they get lost in the details and miss the big picture.

As I said, if I have a genius, it's that I see the fundamental principles in most disciplines that you need to understand in order to apply them to real-life issues. Is this a genius? I don't know, but I believe that you will find that many of life's disciplines can be broken down into very basic concepts.

For example, we don't all have to be accountants, but knowing your personal financial situation is very helpful. I have devoted a chapter of this book to finance because I believe that it is a basic skill that we can all use. Similarly, setting and achieving goals has basic principles, as does developing successful habits and many other disciplines. Once you understand the basic building blocks of a subject, the details fall

1. Finding Your Genius

into place, and as I said earlier, if I have a genius, it's that I see the big picture quickly. I don't have a genius level IQ or a doctorate degree, but this one skill has been an immense help throughout my life.

Now, let's get back to finding your genius, your free-range chicken skill.

Traditionally, when we say the word "genius," we think of someone with a very high IQ. Mensa, for example, is a high IQ society. To be a member of Mensa, your IQ has to be in the top 2% of all people in the world. Albert Einstein or Stephen Hawking, I am sure, would have qualified for Mensa. These gentlemen were geniuses in every sense of the traditional word, but for the purposes of discussion here, I am using the word genius in a much broader sense. I define a genius as someone with an exceptional skill or a life focus who makes a meaningful contribution with this skill or focus. For example, I know a few teachers who are true geniuses with children in their classroom; they seem to have a magic touch with children. Most of us would be overwhelmed at the prospect of facing twenty-five or more students each day, but these teachers handle a class professionally, and the children in their classrooms are happy and love to learn. This is an example of genius using my definition.

Let's look at another example of genius. I know a couple of people who, when faced with a problem, seem to gravitate to the best solution very quickly and have an action plan in mind before the rest of us even have any idea what to do. It's amazing to watch these people, but I'm not even sure what label to put on their genius. They just seem to intuitively see what solutions will work, what won't, and very quickly have a plan of action to get the job done.

I believe that there are hundreds, if not thousands, of types of genius. There are financial geniuses, artistic geniuses, musical geniuses, literary geniuses, and the list goes on and on. The challenge in this complex world is to find your genius and to help others find theirs. For the rest of this chapter, I plan to focus on the challenge of finding your personal genius and how the role of parents, our education system, and society, as a whole, can help develop our hidden geniuses.

Imagine a world where eight billion people are focused on what they do best.

Finding Your Personal Genius

My friend Sam, the free-range chicken, found his genius out of necessity. If he was going to eat regularly, he needed to figure out very quickly how the world worked. Sitting at home and hoping for the best wouldn't get the job done.

Finding your genius is often a challenge. I know that when I graduated from high school, I had no idea what I was going to do. Fortunately, my parents insisted that I go to university. This gave me a few more years to figure out my future direction. At university, I majored in mathematics, but after three years of math, I knew that it wasn't going to be my life's passion. I received very good marks, but math didn't really light a fire in me. I finished my degree with a major in math, but after graduating, I got my first full-time job in one of the few computer centers in the city and ended up spending my whole career in the information technology field, working my way up from technical positions to senior management and senior sales roles. Technology wasn't my genius, but despite my early misgivings, I found that I was quite good at and enjoyed sales. I learned very early that if people like you trust you and respect you, they will do business with you. I'm sure that this is true for all professions.

I'm realize that my story is very common. Serendipity plays a bigger role in our life than most of us realize. Life just seems to happen without as much conscious thought as should have been given. For example, think back to a couple of big decisions that you made. What if you hadn't taken that new job? What about moving to that new city? How different would your life have been if you had made a few key decisions differently?

Also, keep in mind that your life passion, your genius, does not necessarily translate into your career and that's OK. I was at a bank the other day and noticed that the loan officer had a fine arts degree diploma hanging on her wall. When I asked her about her background

Table of Contents

1. Finding Your Genius   1
  Life as a Free-Range Chicken   1
  What's Your Free-Range Chicken Skill?   3
  Finding Your Personal Genius   6
    Risk Taking   7
    The Influence of Parents and Immediate Family   8
    Our Education System   9
  Lessons in This Book   10
    Successful Habits   10
    Goal Setting   10
    Finance   11
    Health and Wellness   11
    Productivity   12
    Religion and Moral Code   12
    Time Management   12
  Summary   13

2. Successful Habits   15
  Why Are Habits Important?   15
  Habits and Productivity   17
    To-Do Lists   18
    Setting Priorities   18
    One-Touch System   19
    80/20 Principle   20
    Being Proactive   20
    Goal Setting   21
    Building on Your Strengths   21
    Avoiding Time Wasters   22
    Persevering   22

Habits and Health and Wellness	23
Exercise	24
Diet	24
Balance	25
Habits and Finances	25
Kicking Bad Habits	26
Mundane Bad Habits	26
Bad Mental Habits	27
Summary	28
Quotes	29
Appendix A *My Management Ten Commandments*	30
3. Goal Setting	**32**
Why Is Goal Setting Important?	32
Three Ingredients in Achieving Your Goals	33
SMART Objectives	34
Action Plans	35
Weight Loss Example	36
Sports Example	37
Finance Example	38
Health and Wellness Example	39
Intellectual Example	40
Short Term Goals for the Day or Week	41
One-Touch System	42
Become a Hard Thinker	42
Other Ways to Achieve Your Goals	43
Summary	44
4. Finance	**46**
Why Is Understanding Your Finances Important?	46
Financial Literacy	47
Growing Your Income	49
Slow-and-Steady Growth of Your Net Worth	50
The Magic of Compound Interest	51
Stock Market Average Returns	53
Common Investment Mistakes	54

The FIRE System—Financial Independence Retire Early	56
Our Financial Story	56
What Would I Do Differently?	57
Reducing Your Discretionary Spending	58
How Long Will My Money Last?	59
Summary and Next Steps to Complete Your Financial Planning	60
Example One—Setting Up a TFSA	61
Example Two—Setting Up a RRSP	62
Example Three—Reducing Discretionary Spending	63
Final Thoughts on Finance	65
Resources You May Find Helpful	66
Quotes You May Enjoy	66
Appendix B *Financial Dos, Don'ts, and Important Information*	**68**
Appendix C *TFSA Contribution Limits*	**71**
Appendix D *RRSP Contribution Rules*	**72**
5. Health and Wellness	**74**
Why Should Health and Wellness Be a Priority?	74
Know Your Own Health First	76
The Seven Key Ingredients to Health and Wellness	77
Nutrition	78
Exercise	79
Sleep and Rest	81
Social Interaction	81
Mental Health	82
Sense of Purpose	86
Balance	86
Summary	87
Suggested Reading	88
6. Productivity	**89**
Why Is Being Productive So Important?	89
Focus on Your Priorities	90

Your Habits Are Key	90
Occam's Razor	91
Productivity Habits and Tools	92
Key Priorities	93
Build on Your Strengths	93
Get Help from Good People	94
Persistent Action	95
Productivity Boosters and Productivity Compounding	96
Avoid Just Being Busy—Busy Work Is a Productivity Killer	97
Avoid Multi-Tasking	98
Limit Social Media	98
Summary	98
Finally, a few quotes that may inspire you:	100
7. Religion and Moral Code	**101**
What Is Your Moral Code?	101
Biblical Stories Are Troubling	102
The Virgin Birth	103
Noah and the Ark	103
Jonah and the Whale	103
Common Religious Expressions that Trouble Me	104
The Story of Creation Is Also Deeply Troubling	104
Cafeteria Christians	105
Other Humans in the Homo Genus	105
Thousands of Gods	106
My Personal Moral Code	106
The Ten Commandments—A Christian Moral Code?	107
Summary	108
8. Time Management	**110**
How Can You Successfully Manage Your Time?	110
Do It, Delegate It, or Drop It	111
Get Your Priorities In Order	111
Just Get Started	111
Use Technology	112
Use the 80/20 Principle (Pareto Principle)	113

Use Occam's Razor	113
Motivate Yourself—Keep Track of Your Progress and Reward Yourself	114
Become an Early Riser	114
Exercise	114
Try Parkinson's Law	115
Consider Parkinson's Law of Triviality	115
Plan for Murphy's Law	115
Take Ownership	116
Miscellaneous Time Management Thoughts	116
Compounding Time Management	117

9. Play It Again Sam — 119

Find Your Genius—People Skills May Be the Answer	119
Like, Trust, and Respect	120
Communication Skill	121
Listening Skill	121
Empathy	121
Health and Wellness	122
Successful Habits	122
Goals	123
Finance	123
Religion and Moral Code	124
Personal Responsibility	124
Keys to a Happy and Successful Life—It all Boils Down to This!	124

and suggested that an artistic banker was unusual, she just laughed and said that she liked living in a house and not her car. Her art was still a passion, but life forced her to make compromises. This is true for many people. Think about the accountant whose passion is coaching hockey or the teacher who plays guitar in a band on the weekend. Life's demands required that their genius and passion take a backseat to fulfilling more basic life requirements—but they still manage to give their genius the priority it deserves.

Risk Taking

Often, in order to find your genius, you must be prepared to put yourself "out there" and take risks. I am the grandfather of seven grandchildren, and I've had many proud and amazing moments from all of them, but one incident in particular absolutely blew my mind.

Our middle granddaughter's school was having a talent day. On talent day, the children would perform their particular talent in front of the whole school and later in front of hundreds of parents and family. Our eight-year-old granddaughter came home from school one day and announced that since the teacher said she couldn't demonstrate her hockey stick-handling skills, she was going to sing at talent day. When her parents asked, in amazement, what song she was going to sing, she replied that she wasn't sure yet. Her plan was to search for a song that she liked on the internet. She found a song, practised, and sang beautifully at talent day, even though she had never done anything like that before. I don't know about you, but I would never have been able to do this at any time in my life, and certainly not when I was eight years old. Our granddaughter is now taking guitar lessons and singing. Who knows where this will lead. The point is that she took a risk and found a talent we didn't know she had.

Keep in mind that you are only taking a risk when you have something to lose. That something might be monetary, but in most cases, it is not. Often what holds us back is the fear of failure. For example, I've had an idea for this book for many years but didn't take the risk for fear that I would fail. The COVID-19 pandemic provided the time, and to be brutally honest, the need to overcome the boredom of isolation was greater than my fear of failure. I don't know if this book will ever be successful, but taking the risk of writing it has given me a great deal of satisfaction and has filled many satisfying hours.

📝 Your homework is to take a few minutes to think about risk taking in your life. Is there something that you have neglected?

The Influence of Parents and Immediate Family

Parents and immediate family are the first line of creativity in the challenge of helping children find their life's passion. This isn't a role that parents should take lightly, as is illustrated by the story of a friend of ours who wanted to be a doctor but was discouraged by her father, who told her that she wasn't "smart enough." She did become a very respected medical professional but to this day regrets not becoming a doctor as a result of her father's discouragement.

I have had the pleasure of seeing the genius of my three children, their spouses, and seven grandchildren. All have unique skills that, in the case of my children, I had the pleasure of watching develop through their formative years. All three, like their mother, have outstanding people skills and all have an additional "genius" that has made them very successful in their chosen fields. By their mid teens, not surprisingly, it was clear to their mother and me what direction their career path would take.

It's been said that it takes a village to raise a child. In today's modern world, I'm sure that isn't often literally true anymore, but our society and culture does provide the framework for our children to develop their talent. In the not-too-distant past, a child's direct influencers didn't extend much beyond their immediate family and their teacher, but a child raised today is bombarded with influence through the internet, TV, and social media as well as the traditional family influence. This opens many more doors in which to find your genius but can also lead to information and option overload. Combine this with helicopter parents filling every waking minute with structured time for sports, school, art, music, and you may find a child with too many options and too little time to develop their talent.

First, a word of caution, don't pigeon hole your children by forcing them down one path at the expense of all others. Children, especially in their early years, must be given a chance to explore and try a few avenues. Finding your genius is not linear, and the genius of a child is not necessarily the same as the genius of the parents.

Our Education System

My family has a great many professional educators. The first, that I am aware of, was my great aunt who was the dean of women at a private high school. She put my father through university, where he obtained two degrees and taught and became the principal of the school that I attended. In addition, I have a Bachelor of Education degree and taught for seven years, plus my wife, daughter, oldest son, and sister are, or were, teachers. I make this point only to suggest that education is a topic that I have a great deal of experience with, both directly and indirectly, through family. Believe me, teachers talk about their job, so I know about the challenges.

First, a few words about the progress that we have made in our education system. When I was in high school, the focus was, almost exclusively, on preparing students for university. As I explained earlier, my father was the principal. He also taught several senior classes and was an outstanding teacher, but he admitted years later, that his focus was far too narrow. When we graduated, we were ready to tackle university, or at least as ready as a student from a small town could be. At that time, only a small percentage of us went on to higher education. There were no senior art, music, or technical vocational courses and certainly no encouragement to "find our genius." It may seem that I am being rather hard on my father and the education system that helped shape me; however, they did the best that they could, within the constraints of the education system of that time, and most of their students did very well. The focus was very narrow, but it was delivered with excellence.

Teachers are often the second line of support, after parents, for a child to find his or her genius. If you are a teacher, don't take this role lightly. I taught at a post-secondary institution for seven years, and in thinking back, it was easy to recognize those students with outstanding technical skills, but far more difficult to recognize those with exceptional "softer" non-technical skills. For example, those with excellent communication and people skills. These students, more often than not, were very successful as well.

Lessons in This Book

Like most of you, I have learned many of life's lessons the slow, painful way, and as a result, I'm writing this book to document what I've learned. Sam, the free-range chicken, taught me one very important lesson about the importance of people skills, but once you have found your genius, your free-range chicken skill, there are still a number of other key concepts you should think about. I've written a chapter on each and summarized them below.

Successful Habits

Successful people have successful habits. This is as straight forward as I can say it, as your habits will have a profound impact on your health, your finances, your relationships, and all other areas of your life.

If you find your genius, find a life partner you love and who loves you, and have successful habits, I can almost guarantee that you will have a very successful life.

Goal Setting

Countless books have been written on the topic of setting and achieving your goals, but for the purposes of most people, all you really need to do is set SMART objectives and have an action plan to achieve them. For most people and most goals, the action plan does not need to be more complicated than a list of steps. I will deal with SMART objectives and action plans later, but for now all you need to remember is that a goal without an action plan is just a dream. There is a price to pay in order to achieve your goals, and you must be willing to pay the price.

Finance

Finance is another topic that makes most people's eyes glaze over, but keep in mind that the basic concepts that you need to understand in the financial world are very simple. For example, the Rule of 72 is a rule of thumb that you can use to determine how quickly your investment will double in value if you know the interest rate. I will explain this in detail in Chapter 4, but once you understand the magic of compound interest, you will be amazed at how your investments will grow. In the finance section of this book, I will outline some simple guidelines that will help you get your financial world in order. In the world of finance, there is a silver bullet: you have to setup a system to pay yourself first. Life really isn't all that complicated, but you do have to think and organize your financial world.

Health and Wellness

Health and wellness is another topic that is, of course, extremely important, but unfortunately, in the day-to-day stress of life, it is often neglected. Both my wife and I have had health scares and, as a result, are very conscious about the very simple but important steps that we can take to stay healthy. You have no control over your genes and sometimes limited control over your environment, but you do control what you eat and drink and how much you exercise. Personal accountability is another topic that I feel very strongly about. You are responsible for your health and wellness, so get off your behind and take control of your life.

Productivity

We have all met people who seem to be unbelievably productive. They seem to be able to get more done in an hour than most people accomplish in a day, and it isn't immediately obvious how they do it. In some cases, this skill has been developed over many years and is, in fact, their genius, but often this talent is nothing more than a fanatical focus on the job at hand. They see through to the essence of what they are trying to accomplish and refuse to be distracted.

I have a couple of people in my immediate family who are amazingly productive, and I'm still amazed when I see them in action, but keep in mind that there are tools and habits that can help the rest of us become more productive.

Religion and Moral Code

Religion is another insanely complex topic that thousands of books have covered in far more detail than I am prepared to do. However, it seems to me that the first question to ask is, do you believe in a supreme being who created the heavens and the earth? If you do, then do some meaningful research, pick a religion that aligns with your values, and live your life accordingly. If you do not believe in a supreme being, you have a little more work to do. You have to create your own personal moral code and live your life in alignment with your code. Now, before you get all bent out shape thinking about your personal moral code, keep in mind that your moral code can be as simple as deciding that you are going to treat everyone the way you want to be treated. My personal moral code is a little more detailed, as I will outline in Chapter 7. Remember, life really isn't all that complicated, but you really should think about how you want to live your life.

Time Management

We can't manage time in any meaningful way in the same manner that we manage money, but there are a great many techniques that we can use to accomplish more with the time that we have. Keep in mind that even if you live to be a 100 years old, you will only have approximately 5,200 weeks in your life, and we all have 24 hours a day and 600 minutes in even a 10-hour workday. We can't change any of this, but we can make much better use of the limited time that we have.

Summary

By now, I hope that you are getting the message that life really isn't all that complicated. It does, however, require you to accept personal responsibility for how you live your life and to think about some basic concepts and how you can apply them.

As I said earlier, if I have a genius, its that I see things a little differently than most people. I try to break concepts down to their basic components and, if needed, work with the details as required. From a very early age, I applied two principles that when I was young, I could not have put a name to but, nevertheless, used them.

First is the 80/20 Principle, which suggests that 20% of the inputs results in 80% of the outputs or results. Even in high school, I can remember thinking through the curriculum very carefully in order to maximize my results (i.e., grades) with the limited time that I had to cram for an exam. I was very busy with most sports, and as a result, studying played second fiddle. My father was the school principal; good grades were expected, and the 80/20 Principle helped me achieve them.

Second is Occam's razor, which is a heuristic, or rule of thumb, that states that when everything else is equal, the solution that makes the fewest assumptions is most often the correct one. This is often the simplest and most straightforward answer. This concept proved invaluable early in my career in the information technology industry. When we had a problem with our computer systems, the first issue that I followed up on was the last change that we had made to the application. More often than not, the source of the problem was found in the code for the last change. Despite the fact that I could not put a name to the principle that I was using, Occam's razor proved invaluable throughout my career since I always looked for the simplest solution first.

In the chapters to follow, I will outline these topics, and others in more detail, but I will try to keep simplicity top-of-mind. This isn't rocket science, and I am not trying to impress you. I sincerely hope when you have finished reading this book, that you think to yourself that, in fact, all the topics covered were really simple because they are. Most complex topics can be broken down into very easy-to-understand principles.

Einstein said that if you can't explain something in simple terms, you don't understand it well enough. I'm certainly not in Einstein's league, but I hope that you find this book easy to read and understand.

📝 Your homework is to think carefully about your personal genius and how you can leverage it in the future.

2. Successful Habits

"Successful people are simply those with successful habits."
— BRIAN TRACY

Why Are Habits Important?

This is by far the most important chapter in this book, as so much of your life is dependent on your habits, including your health, your productivity, and your financial position, to name just a few.

Your habits have the power to change you from who you are to who you want to become. Unfortunately, as many have discovered, your habits also have the power to shorten your life, ruin relationships, destroy your health, and bankrupt you financially. The objectives of this chapter are to explain and illustrate how habits work and to outline several positive habits that have made a big difference in my life.

Habits can control your life if you let them. Here is a simple example: For the last four years, the first thing I do in the morning is have a cup of coffee and read the local paper online. While writing this book, I had been trying to change this habit for many months. I am most productive in the morning, so I wanted to work on this book for the first few hours of the morning and read the paper later, but making the change was a challenge. As soon as I had my coffee in my hand, I'd automatically go to my computer and read the online paper. It was just a small habit, but it was a challenge to change. To help me make this change, I placed a printed copy of the table of contents of this book beside my computer every night as a reminder. In the morning, this forced me to think about my decision—should I read the paper or work on this book? This worked, but I needed this reminder to assist me and I didn't have my coffee reward until I had written at least a paragraph. This is just a very small and mundane habit, but it illustrates how we are all truly creatures of habit.

The pandemic has certainly changed all our lives and forced us to create new habits. Wearing a mask when leaving the condo is a habit that my wife and I have struggled with. Not that we don't believe that masks help control the spread of the virus, we just had difficulty adopting this new habit. My wife came up with a reminder to help us: she hung a mask on the handle of the door so we couldn't miss it. In the past, we often ended up in the car without a mask. Now we wear a mask every time we leave the condo.

Reminders are the first lesson in this chapter on habits. Here are a few more examples of reminders that may help you create positive new habits:

- To help you start a morning exercise program, set out your clothes and shoes the night before and set them out where you have to move them to get to the bathroom.
- Put a big note on your fridge door reminding you of your diet so that when you go to the fridge for a snack, you are reminded that you have given up snacks.
- To help you remember that internet addiction is a very bad habit, put your phone away for certain hours of the day and have your phone automatically send you a reminder to put it away during your restricted hours.

You get the idea. Reminders will help you develop new habits or break old ones.

Habits form in a three-part process according to the experts: reminder, behaviour, and reward. Of course, if it truly is to be a habit, repeat must be part of the process.

Let's look again at my old habit of reading the paper online in the morning. In the past, as soon as I sat down at my desk, I automatically went to the online paper and had my coffee. To change this habit, I needed a reminder about my new habit, which was placing the table of contents for this book on my desk by the computer; my new behaviour was writing online, and the reward was my morning coffee, which I didn't make until I had written at least a paragraph. I love my morning coffee, so it is a very meaningful reward, but this new habit still didn't completely form.

Habits take time to form and the "reminder, behaviour, reward" sequence does work, but there is no magic timeframe. It depends on the person and the habit being formed. Personally, I have found that it really helps if I have a reminder that I absolutely cannot ignore; I have made it very easy to initiate the new action and have a small but meaningful reward. For me, after about a month, most habits are ingrained. However, if I slip and fall back into the old behaviour, all my progress is lost very quickly.

We don't think of many of our every day actions as habits. We are just on autopilot and do them without thinking. Driving a car is a good example. When we first learned to drive, we had to think of each step in the correct order and were very focused on the process, but after a short period of time, this became automatic. This chapter is not going to cover this type of habit but will examine some broad habit categories that will help you become more productive, healthier, and wealthier. This is a tall order, but if you are trying to change a habit, start small and use the reminder and reward system. It works.

Habits and Productivity

Productivity is such an important topic that I have dedicated a complete chapter of this book to it, but productivity must also be referenced in this chapter on habits. Successful people are, by definition, more productive, and they are more productive because they have successful habits.

In today's world, everyone seems to be running hard with very little spare time, and as a result, spare time is often the reward for being more productive. I know that it certainly was when I was working full time and helping raise a family. To find more spare time, I used the tools and techniques outlined below. These habits worked for me.

To-Do Lists

A to-do list is a very simple but effective tool that I have used for many years. When I first began using to-do lists, I used paper, but now I keep the list online and reference it many times during the day. The reminder is, of course, the list on my computer and the simple reward that I use is putting a happy face beside the action item once it is complete. A to-do list organizes and sets priorities for your day and should leave you with a sense of accomplishment, not a feeling of defeat, so challenge yourself with your to-do list but don't overwhelm yourself. A typical daily to-do list for me would include action items such as the following:

1. Work on my book for two hours first thing in the morning.
2. Go for a bike ride.
3. Play pickleball for two hours in the afternoon.
4. Make arrangements with our optometrist to have our bi-annual eye test.
5. Visit my mother at 4:00.
6. Read for an hour in the evening.

As I explained, the reward system that I use with my to-do list is putting a happy face after each action item once it is complete. Sounds hokey, but it works for me.

Remember, arranging action items in a to-do list helps reduce stress since you are unlikely to forget them. Procrastination causes stress.

Setting Priorities

Priorities are another key to becoming more productive. Don't fall into the trap of spending your day completing small trivial action items at the expense of the truly important tasks.

I use two tools to keep my priorities in line. The first tool is a list of priorities in the form of resolutions that I make each year. These are the key priorities for the year. I use five categories with several action items in each category. The categories that I have been using for several years are the following:

- homelife
- health
- social
- finance
- charity

I reference my resolutions a couple of times a month and, again, use happy faces by the action items if I am on track and sad faces if I am not. My resolutions are my key priorities for the year.

The second tool is my daily to-do list. My daily to-do list links back to my resolutions as required. For example, one of my resolutions for this year was to find a second charity to support, and my daily to-do list had an action item that involved doing research and, together with my wife, picking a charity. Resolutions without action will fail. At the risk of stating the obvious, you must link the action items in your to-do list back to your high-priority resolutions.

I can almost hear some of you thinking, "Man, this guy is anal." I am—but this system works.

One-Touch System

The one-touch system, as the name implies, means that you handle some action items with one iteration rather than spinning your wheels thinking about it over and over instead of completing the task. For example, if you need to take the garbage out, don't put this action item on your to-do list for the day, just take the darn garbage out. Another example involves the hundreds of work emails that many of us receive in a week. Most can be read and just be deleted and others should be handled with one-touch. If a co-worker asks your opinion on a project, don't write a mini doctoral thesis; just spend a few minutes giving a high-level view in a short reply email.

The one-touch system will save you time and reduce your stress level. Action items that seem to hang around are a terrible stress creator. Don't let this happen to you.

80/20 Principle

Focusing on the 20% of the inputs that yield 80% of the results will, of course, make you far more productive. As a result of compounding, a 15% productivity improvement each month for six months will more than double your productivity. Compounding is an almost magical principle in the financial world, but it works in the same way for self improvement. More on compounding and this principle in chapters 4 and 8, respectively.

Being Proactive

Proactive people take the initiative to make "sh*t" happen. At the risk of being crude, this is really what being proactive is all about. I have a couple of people in my family who are amazingly proactive. They can look at a problem, see several possible solutions, pick the best one, and get the job done before most people even get started. This is an amazing talent that has made them productive and as a result successful. I have watched them perform this "proactive magic" for many years, but I am still not quite sure how they do it. They just seem to quickly see to see through to the heart of an issue and have a strong bias for action.

I'm a proactive person, but I am not in the same league as these people. I use tools to help me be more productive and proactive. Some of the tools that I use are the following, in no particular order:

- to-do lists
- setting priorities
- timelines
- setting goals

2. Successful Habits

- pro and con lists to evaluate alternatives
- research on the internet

My message here is that if you are one of those super proactive people who just seem to make good things happen, more power to you. If you are not, there are tools to help you, but don't get caught in "analysis paralysis."

Goal Setting

I have dedicated a complete chapter to setting and achieving goals, so I am not going to repeat it here. However, you should keep in mind that the three main ingredients involved in achieving your goals are:

- establishing SMART objectives;
- developing action plans; and,
- working your action plans and persevering, persevering, persevering.

Setting and achieving your goals is almost a definition of productivity.

Building on Your Strengths

In my formative years, the prevalent theme was that you must overcome your weaknesses. As I have aged, I have concluded that this, for the most part, is wrong. We should build on our strengths and, as outlined in an earlier chapter, find our genius. You need only overcome weaknesses that impede your strengths or are an absolute requirement to live in today's world.

As an example, I am not at all artistic. In public school, I dreaded art class because I had no innate artistic ability and I knew that my artwork was subpar, to say the least. I had good ideas for my artwork but couldn't deliver on them. It was very stressful. My father was the school principal and good grades were expected. To my parents credit, they cut me some slack in art. As it turned out, my career in IT did not require artistic ability, but nevertheless, this weakness rears its head every now and then in my day-to-day life. I have just learned to live with it.

If you think about the successful people that you know, most of them have developed a small number of skills that made them successful. They have built on their strengths and received help, when required, with their weaknesses. Surgeons, for example, focus on their operating room skills and get help with booking appointments, billing, accounting, and other skills required for a successful medical practice.

Focusing on your strengths will make you far more successful and happier in the long run. Another way of saying this is that you should bet on your strengths and buy your weaknesses. This concept alone will make you more successful in life, especially if you combine it with the 80/20 Principle that states that 20% of your effort produces 80% of the result. Results are what counts in a successful life. If you focus on the key 20%, you will be amazed at the results you can achieve.

Avoiding Time Wasters

We all do many activities that waste hours every day. Emails, texts, and social media are obvious ones that we all know about, but there are others that are more insidious and can really consume your mind and your time. Think about the following:

- Do you worry about issues of the past that you can do nothing about? If so, just let it go.
- Do you worry about other people's issues? If it is out of your control, just let it go.
- Are you trying to maintain relationships with poisonous people? Are they worth it?
- Are you getting help when you need it?

Persevering

Perseverance is another key habit of very successful people. They just don't seem to give up, but it's difficult to define how one becomes a person who perseveres. Is perseverance an innate personality trait? Can it be learned? Is perseverance just a function of fear of failure?

Let's look at the classic example of trying to develop a new morning exercise habit. Getting up an hour earlier in the morning to go for a run or walk is difficult for most of us. We will have many potential excuses, such as work, family commitments, a late night, and so on. The key is to persevere despite occasional setbacks, but it's been my experience that peer pressure and the buddy system help. Tell everyone in your family about your new morning exercise program and talk your significant other into working out with you.

Personally, I have found that my to-do list or an action plan step for one of my goals is an excellent motivator to persevere. As mentioned earlier, I have a habit of putting happy faces 😊 beside completed steps and sad faces ☹ when I give up. Sounds anal, but it works for me. The point is, I hate seeing those sad faces, so they force me to persevere. Your goals will never be realized if you quit, so persevere, persevere, and persevere some more.

The only caution is the riding a dead horse metaphor: sometimes your goal is a dead horse, so just get off and start walking.

Habits and Health and Wellness

It's trite but true to say that without your health, you have very little. My wife and I have both had health scares and know first hand that serious health issues simply consume your life—everything revolves around getting better as quickly as possible. As a result, when you are unwell, often the good habits that you have developed over many years are dropped out of necessity.

There are many possible habits that promote health and wellness. Chapter 5 is devoted to health and wellness, but in this chapter, I only plan to review three key habits: exercise, diet, and finding balance in your life.

Exercise

I have always been a very active person, so exercising is a habit that has come very easy to me. In retirement, I have more free time and exercise an average of 12 to 15 hours a week by walking, biking, golfing, playing pickleball, and completing a morning stretching program. My exercise regime is now second nature to me, and the exercise has become the reward by itself, but it took many years to become this way. The keys for me were repetition and perseverance so that it became a habit. I don't like it when I have to miss exercising, but I don't lay a guilt trip on myself. Life sometimes gets in the way of even the best habits.

Let's get back to the reminder, behaviour, and reward system that we reviewed at the beginning of this chapter. This system will help you develop and persevere with your exercise program. For example, if you want to get up an hour early and go for a walk or run before work, you could set out your running shoes and clothes in the bathroom as a reminder and use your morning coffee as a reward after your run. Further motivation through peer pressure or a buddy system are also good options. Telling your family and friends as well as taking your partner running with you will motivate you to persevere.

Your exercise program should also be fun and match your personality. If you are not a morning person and are very extroverted, a morning walk by yourself will not likely work for you. An after-work group exercise program at the local gym might be a better match for your personality.

A word of caution: if you are overweight or have a serious medical condition, consult with your doctor before starting your exercise program and possibly get professional help from a fitness expert.

Finally, don't give up if you miss a few days of your exercise program. Life can get in the way but persevere, persevere, persevere.

Diet

Diet is an area of my life where I have struggled. I have sweet tooth and find it very hard to resist junk food. My exercise program keeps my weight in line, but I still consume far too many "empty calories." The key for me to cut down on junk food is just to not have any in the house but to always have plenty of fruit and cut-up vegetables. When I need a snack, I don't have any junk-food options, but I do have healthy options.

This isn't a brilliant solution backed by scientific evidence, but it works for me. Out of sight, out of mind, and, most importantly in this case, out of stomach.

Balance

Balance, our third topic under health and wellness, involves more than finding balance between your work life and your home life. Your habits, in large part, determine the balance in your life. Even good habits such as exercise have the power to significantly upset your life balance. I've known people who became obsessed with their running habit at the expense of their family and, in some cases, at the expense of their health. Others have become almost addicted to their saving and financial habits to the extent that they've taken the joy out of life.

Only you, and those closest to you, can examine the balance in your life and determine what might be upsetting this balance. Is it your diet, your work, your cell phone, binge-watching TV, or even a hobby that you have become obsessed with? Talk to those closest to you if you believe that your life needs a tune-up.

Habits and Finances

Good financial habits don't just happen, they are developed over time with discipline and perseverance. Chapter 4 is all about the topic of finance, so I am not going to repeat it all here. Just remember that the slow-and-steady investment growth system outlined in this book requires you to form these three habits:
- determine how much discretionary income you have each month;

- save a set percentage of your discretionary income in a pension fund, TFSA, RRSP, or all three; and,
- watch your investments grow tax-free with time and the magic of compound interest. Remember, investing is a marathon not a sprint.

It is really not that complicated—it's just about making it a habit. Anyone can do it.

Kicking Bad Habits

Habits, in large part, make us who we are. This is true for our good habits and our bad habits. Most habits, however, are neither good nor bad but are simply learned behaviours that we repeat so that we can go on autopilot through a large part of our life. We don't think about taking a shower in the morning, making coffee, or driving a car. We just perform these habits automatically without a great deal of thought.

Kicking a bad habit, however, will require you to think and will involve hard work, perseverance, and often a substitute behaviour. Just telling yourself to change doesn't work for most of us.

I have never smoked and don't drink to excess, so I am not going to attempt to try to tell you how to kick these bad habits. There is professional help available for both—use it.

Mundane Bad Habits

Let's look at a couple of more mundane habits that I have experience with.

First, being a couch potato and binge-watching TV: For me, this is particularly a problem in the winter. The reminder for me is my 5:00 p.m. glass of wine. When I have my wine, I sit down in my reclining chair, watch the early news on TV, then the 6:00 news, and often don't do anything other than watch TV all night. This is a bad habit, not a terrible one, but still one that I would like to change by substituting reading for at least an hour in the evening rather than just mindlessly watching TV. The reminder to get out a book and turn off the TV will be the end of the 5:00 news, and the reward will be my glass of wine.

A second bad habit that I have is checking on the stock market many times during the day. I don't do anything with the information other than worry if the stock market is going down, so checking it ten or twelve times a day is a waste of time. As a friend of mine said one day when I was moaning and groaning about the stock market, "Does that mean that now you can only live to 115 before your money runs out?" This put things in perspective for me. In order to stop checking the market so often, I'm simply going to make it more difficult to do so by removing the link from my list of favourites. My reward, I hope, will be more peace of mind.

Bad Mental Habits

Finally, let's take a quick look at a few mental bad habits that I have experience with.

The first is repeating the same mistake over and over and not learning from your mistakes. My dad used to say that life was far too short and there are far too many possible mistakes to just learn from your own mistakes. You must learn from the mistakes of others. So, there are two lessons here: not repeating your own mistakes, and becoming a student of human nature and learning from the missteps of others.

The classic example that I have observed is failed weight-loss programs that focus on an unusual diet but neglect exercise. I am a big believer in a holistic weight-loss approach that combines sensible eating with an exercise program tailored to the needs of the individual. I have seen far too many fad diets that caused nothing but stress in the lives of those trying them. There is no silver bullet for weight loss.

The second mental bad habit that I personally am guilty of is reluctance to change even when I know that change is required. I am a creature of habit, and as a result, anything outside of my daily habits causes me a great deal of stress. For example, my local gym recently closed. This forced me to adjust my workout routine, and you would think that I would simply find a new gym or develop a workout routine at home, but the process was stressful and took months before I accepted the result. There is an old saying that if your horse dies, get off and start walking. Most of us try to get the dead horse up and moving long after we should have been walking. This metaphor applies to many of our significant life upheavals.

Think about the possible dead horses in your life.

The third mental bad habit that I have is worrying about things that I have no control over or, worse still, worrying about and reliving my past mistakes by mulling over the brilliant things I would've liked to have said and done rather than the mundane things I actually said and did. My solution to both problems is to simply sit down and document the issue and what I learned from the past mistake or, if I am worried about a future problem, document the problem and possible steps to mitigate the issue. For example, if I am worried that the stock market is going to suffer a serious correction, I plan to write down the steps that I can take with my portfolio to mitigate my risk. I can't control the stock market, but I have some control over my personal financial portfolio.

Summary

There is a science behind breaking bad habits and creating new ones. The science involves three components: a reminder to initiate the new habit; the action/behaviour of the habit itself; and a reward for doing the new habit. My simple, almost trivial, example of replacing my habit of reading the paper first in the morning and replacing it with working on this book involved a reminder to initiate the new habit (the table of contents for the book placed beside my computer the night before), the behaviour of initiating writing the book first thing in the morning, and a reward (my coffee) after I have written a paragraph. This is a very simple example that involved changing one habit for another. My habit of reading the paper first thing in the morning wasn't really a bad habit, but it was one that I wanted to change.

2. Successful Habits

I truly believe that good habits will make you more successful and bad habits have the power to shorten your life, ruin relationships, destroy your health, and bankrupt you financially.

If you don't remember anything else from this book, remember that good habits are the keys to your success and bad habits are the road to failure. Life is not that complicated.

📝 Your homework is to pick one habit that you wish to change using the "reminder, behaviour, and reward" system.

Quotes

Here are a few quotes on habits that I found online that may resonate with you:

"If your habits don't line up with your dream, then you need to either change your habits or change your dream."
— JOHN C. MAXWELL

"Good habits are the key to all success. Bad habits are the unlocked door to failure."
— OG MANDINGO

"Successful people aren't born that way. They became successful by establishing the habit of doing things unsuccessful people don't like to do."
— WILLIAM MAKEPEACE THACKERAY

"Most of us have uphill dreams and downhill habits."
— AUTHOR UNKNOWN

Appendix A
My Management Ten Commandments

These are not strictly speaking habits, but I had a habit of referencing them frequently during my work career and they certainly helped me become successful.

1. Know your customers and their requirements extremely well. Your customers are the key to your success.
2. Understand your financial statements inside and out. You won't be in business long if you don't show a profit.
3. Hold your staff accountable. Perfection isn't required but dedication, accountability, and perseverance are.
4. Use the one-touch system whenever possible. In other words, handle things immediately and only once. Issues that hang around waste time and cause stress.
5. Managements by procrastination is sometimes an alternative. This contradicts step four above, but some issues/projects should just be left to simmer in the hope that they go away. Only you can reasonably judge which projects should be handled immediately and which should not be handled at all.
6. If you focus on the actions, the goals will take care of themselves.
7. It is important to be a hard worker but equally important to be a hard thinker.

Appendix A   My Management Ten Commandments

8. Planning improves performance. Even to-do lists help but repetitive tasks in a business setting should have a written process. A follow-up to this rule is that poor planning by someone else should not create an emergency for you.
9. Learn to say, "No," but if you see someone who is clearly very stressed, offer to help. People are still number one.
10. Very few things in life are worth losing sleep over. Ask yourself, "Will this be important a year from now?" If not, just do your best and move on.

3. Goal Setting

"Goal setting is not only about choosing the rewards that you want to enjoy, but also the costs that you are willing to pay."
— JAMES CLEAR

Why Is Goal Setting Important?

Goal setting and action plans go hand-in-hand, but most people and many companies just don't get it. I'm a golfer, so I am going to use a simple golf example to illustrate this point. Let's take two amateur golfers, Bob and Mary. Both golfers, for the last five years, have shot an average score of about 95 for 18 holes of golf, and both want to reduce their average score to 90 for the month of September, approximately five months away. This a reasonably good SMART objective, as it is specific (S), measurable (M), attainable (A), realistic (R), and has a timeline (T). Bob was very vocal about his goal and told all his golf buddies. When asked how he was going to do this, he replied that he was going to "golf better." Mary, on the other hand, was also planning to "golf better," but knew that in order to meet her goal, she would have to make changes to her golf game. Her plan included weekly lessons and weekly practise time on the green and driving range as well as playing at least three times a week while tracking her scores. She was willing to pay the price required to improve her golf game and understood that golf objectives, as with all life's objectives, requires hard work, discipline, and perseverance. A goal without an action plan

3. Goal Setting

is just a dream, and Mary was willing to pay the price required to achieve her goal.

Now let's look at another common weakness—too many goals in an unrealistic time frame. I worked for information technology companies for almost my whole career, and I noticed another significant flaw in the goal-setting system used by most companies. At one company I worked for, at the beginning of the year, we would set objectives and then categorize them as "A," "B," "C," and so on. Soon some of the "A's" became "Super A's," meaning that they were even more important than the regular "A's." No objectives were ever dropped, and soon we had a huge number of goals but no coherent plan to follow up, link them, and ensure that all had appropriate action plans. I soon learned that only the "Super A's" deserved any of my time. The moral of the story is that most of us can only realistically hope to work on a few goals at a time, and for most of us, that means one major goal at a time.

Before publication, my personal goal was to complete a draft of this book in one year. Knowing me at the time, you could've argued, quite reasonably, that this was not realistic, as I have a wife and family that I love and want to spend time with. Furthermore, I had never written a book before and had very little idea of all the steps involved from initial draft to publication. In short, I didn't know what I didn't know.

Three Ingredients in Achieving Your Goals

I have been involved with project management for almost all of my career, but it was only in last approximately fifteen years of a forty-four-year career that I achieved any professional project management designations. In the IT company that I retired from, there was a big push to have certified project managers, and as a result, I certified as a project management professional, executive project manager, and project executive. To be brutally honest, I'm not sure that any of these professional designations helped me manage projects better, but they certainly looked good on my resume.

I fully understand that for large complex projects such as large construction projects and large software development projects, stringent project management disciplines are required to deliver quality results on time and on budget. However, for most of our day-to-day work, simple spreadsheets or to-do lists are all that are required.

I have seen projects that focus more on the project management disciplines than on achieving quality results in the given time and budget. I have also seen other projects that ended in analysis paralysis; the project just seemed to go on-and-on with further in-depth review of each micro step.

This chapter won't make you a certified project manager, but it should help you achieve your personal life goals.

For the rest of this chapter, I will focus on what I consider to be the three main ingredients in achieving your goals:

1. SMART objectives;

2. Action plans linked with rewards and fun; and,

3. Working your action plans and persevering.

Finally, I am going to close this chapter with several examples that you may find helpful.

Let's get started.

SMART Objectives

Establishing SMART objectives sets the parameters for the work that you are about to undertake. I did not invent the concept of SMART objectives. In fact, if you do a search on the Internet, you will find SMART templates for a great many goals.

- SMART is of course an acronym. It stands for:
- Specific
- Measurable
- Attainable
- Relevant and Realistic
- Timeline focused

3. Goal Setting

Let's look at each in turn and discuss what they should and should not be.

Specific means, for example, that if you are trying to lose weight, it's not enough to just say you are going to lose weight. You have to specify, among other things, how many pounds you are going to lose.

Measurable, of course, means that you have a way to quantify your weight loss. A bathroom scale is the obvious answer for weight loss.

Attainable, *realistic*, and *relevant*, in my mind, work together. Using the weight loss example again, losing ten pounds a week for ten weeks would be neither attainable nor realistic. One or two pounds a week for ten weeks would seem to be attainable and realistic for most people.

A *timeline* establishes the time parameters for your objective. Using the weight loss example again, the timeline could be a specific end date or interim check points, such as the two pounds per week lost over ten weeks. Multiple check points in a project provide you with additional information you may require to achieve your ultimate goal.

Action Plans

Action plans outline the work that is required to achieve your SMART objectives. Put another way, it is the price that you are willing to pay.

This is where the rubber meets the road. Action plans require thought, planning, hard work, and perseverance. In many cases, it also requires that you know what will work for you and your lifestyle and what will not. For example, if I was to decide to lose two pounds a week for ten weeks and one of the line items in my action plan was to get up at 5:00 a.m. for an early morning one hour swim, I know that I would be doomed to failure. I am a morning person, but not for exercise that early, and I hate swimming. A one-hour bike ride at 7:00 would work much better for me.

Let's look at some realistic examples, keeping the 80/20 Principle in mind in order to maximize our results.

Weight Loss Example

A weight loss example is one that most of us can relate to. Let's assume that our SMART objective is to lose two pounds per week for ten weeks and that our action plan involves both diet and exercise (the calories in/calories out formula). My action plan would include the following:

1. Weigh in every morning when I first get up and record the results in a spreadsheet or equivalent system.
2. Exercise for at least an hour a day, six days a week. In my case, I would ride a bike outside when possible; otherwise, I would use the stationary bike in the bedroom. Most of us don't have time to go to gym six days a week, but we can find time to bike or walk from home.
3. Find a buddy (your spouse or significant other) to help keep you on track.
4. Drink six large glasses of water each day.
5. Eliminate all high calorie drinks, such as soda pop from my diet.
6. Eliminate all desserts and snacks. I have a sweet tooth, so I have found from experience that I can lose a pound a week just through my normal exercise program and by eliminating all cookies, pies, and so on as well as snacks.
7. Eliminate all food between the fourteen hours of 6:00 p.m. to 8:00 a.m. Sounds drastic, but once you get used to the routine, it's quite easy to do.
8. Finally, you must persevere! If you slip and gain a pound or two, don't give up.

This simple system works for me, but you may have to revise it to suit your personal preferences and lifestyle.

Finally, a word of caution. If your doctor has advised you that you are seriously overweight and as a result have, or could have, underlying health issues, then get professional help. This will likely include your doctor and a health/fitness coach.

3. Goal Setting

Sports Example

When I was younger, I played numerous sports, but in retirement, I walk, ride my bike, golf, and play pickleball. I try to get two to three hours of exercise each day for at least five days a week. This isn't practical for everyone, but in retirement, it works for me. When I was working full time, the best that I could ever do was an hour a day, three or four times a week.

I took up pickleball in just the last few years, and while I didn't formally learn the game through a rigorous goal setting/project management process, I did seriously try to get better and took steps to improve, but as you will see, I didn't have a SMART objective. Initially, my only objective was to try the game to see if I liked it.

I went through an ad hoc process that included the following steps:

1. Buying cheap paddles just to get started.
2. Going to a drop in pickleball centre numerous times to try out the game.
3. Watching countless YouTube pickleball videos to learn the basics.
4. Taking a formal beginner lesson.
5. More practice at drop-in centres.
6. Watching more videos and even taking notes.
7. Taking a more advanced lesson.
8. Buying a better paddle.
9. Finding a drop-in centre where I felt comfortable playing with people of similar ability.
10. Playing twice a week for three hours.

This was not a formal project with a defined SMART objective, but I did learn to play pickleball and I am having fun. From previous experience with many other sports, I knew that getting my butt kicked at pickleball would not be fun, so I was determined to improve.

Some projects, such as this one, are more ad hoc in nature, but nevertheless, if you give them some thought, the outcome will improve.

Finance Example

Finance has long been an interest of mine. My latest financial project involved setting up a new tax-free savings account (TFSA). A TFSA, as the name implies, allows your money to both grow and be withdrawn tax free. I have had a TFSA for many years but, in retirement, have not made any deposits for a number of years and, as a result, have unused TFSA deposit room.

My SMART objective was to:

- set up a new TFSA with a leading online broker, according to MoneySense ratings;
- have a balanced investment portfolio managed by this online broker;
- have low expenses related to the account (MER less than 0.5%);
- make monthly deposits of $500 from my checking account; and,
- accomplish the above in less than a week.

My action plan included the following steps:

1. Research MoneySense.ca ratings of online brokers: I found that Questrade was rated number one in 2019 and number two in 2020.
2. Log into Questrade and set up a TFSA with them using one of their predefined options for a balanced fund: This was more complex than I had anticipated and required a few iterations, a few calls to their help desk, and a great deal of patience and perseverance. Their online system is not intuitive, or perhaps the issues that I encountered were just due to my lack of familiarity with their system.
3. Calculate the MER (management expense ratio) for my new TFSA: I found out this is 0.39%, well within my objective.

3. Goal Setting

4. Log into my online bank checking account and fund my new TFSA initially with $1000 (minimum requirement with Questrade) as well as create a monthly recurring deposit of $500 from my checking account to my new TFSA.

All of this took a little longer than a week due to a few false starts and Questrade help desk calls. This project was successful but frustrating. Perseverance was a definite requirement.

Health and Wellness Example

Approximately twenty years ago, at my annual medical checkup, my doctor informed me that my cholesterol was high, and he recommended that I take medication for the condition. I am very averse to any drugs, and so I proceeded to try to convince him to let me try diet and exercise to lower my cholesterol to a normal range. Since my condition was not life threatening, he agreed to let me give diet and exercise a try for six months, provided that I agreed to take the medication prescribed after six months if my diet and exercise program was not successful.

My SMART objective was to lower my cholesterol to the normal range, as outlined by my doctor, within six months. This objective was specific, measurable, and had a timeline, but as it turned out was not attainable or realistic.

I was determined to lower my cholesterol and put an action plan in place that involved diet and exercise. I lost approximately twenty pounds, but my cholesterol did not go down and I have been on the cholesterol medication for about twenty years. The good news is that my wife said that as a result of the diet and exercise, I lost my "shelf" (my gut hanging over my belt).

I didn't achieve my objective but was healthier for trying.

Intellectual Example

The final example of setting and achieving goals that I will use is writing this book. I had never written a book before so I had no idea of the appropriate timeline, the steps involved, possible issues, and so on. We have all been in uncharted territory before, so we just dive in with the knowledge that we have and fine tune the project plan as required.

Obviously, I had a few ideas percolating in my mind before I began the formal process of writing. For example, I knew the title of the book would be *Life Really Isn't All That Complicated, But You Do Have to Think*. I also had ten chapters in mind, so even before I committed to this project, I had an outline in my mind.

The SMART objective was to complete this book of approximately 150 pages and 10 chapters and publish it by December 31, 2022. As earlier stated, I had no idea if this was attainable or realistic but it was specific, measurable, and included a timeline. Now, my action plan in place was to follow the steps below and persevere.

1. Create a table of contents listing the ten chapters that have been percolating in my mind for the last few months.
2. Create a draft of the possible topics for each chapter.
3. Resolve to write for a minimum of ten hours each week.
4. Create an online system to track the number of hours written each day to monitor my progress of achieving my target of writing ten hours per week.
5. In recognition of the fact that this was all new to me, establish interim completion goals such as:
    - complete a first draft of a chapter every month starting in April 1, 2021;
    - complete a second draft of each chapter every month starting January 1, 2022;
    - receive an editorial review (wife and daughter) as chapters are written;
    - complete a final draft of the complete book over the spring and summer; and,

3. Goal Setting

- research the publication process and submit the book to publishers in the fall.
6. Fine tune the action plan as required and persevere! Persevere! Persevere!

This project is classic example of a project that is completely in uncharted territory for me, and as a result, I didn't know what I didn't know. I fully realized that the action plan was sketchy, but I didn't know want to get caught up in "analysis paralysis," so I decided to fine tune as I learned more about writing and publishing a book. If I write a second book, the action plan will be far more comprehensive.

Short Term Goals for the Day or Week

I tend to procrastinate on short-term, non-urgent goals, so as a result of that, I have come up with a system that forces me to make a conscious decision every day as to whether I am going to make progress on a goal. I have found that if I just record the goal on my to-do list, it might sit there for a very long time as a single-line item. However, if I list the goal on my to-do list and, underneath it, list the half a dozen steps in the action plan required to complete it, it gets done much faster. For example, if my short-term goal is to paint the shed, I might record it in my to-do list as follows:

- Goal—paint the shed:
    1. Decide on a colour after discussion with my wife.
    2. Purchase a gallon of paint and a quart of primer.
    3. Prepare the shed for priming and painting.
    4. Prime the bar spots.
    5. Paint the shed.

I know what steps are required to paint the shed and really don't have to write them down, but this system works for me because my to-do list has interim steps and I get the satisfaction of completing the interim steps and using my happy face 😊 system beside each one.

41

Now let's look at two more topics that have helped me reach my goals: the one-touch system and becoming a hard thinker as well as a hard worker.

One-Touch System

The one-touch system is another great time saver, because as the name implies, you do tasks with one-touch rather than multiple iterations. This system works well for a couple of reasons. First, procrastination causes stress. The fact that you know that you have left something undone will weigh on your mind and cause problems in other areas of your life. Second, many of the items on your to-do list can easily be checked off in one iteration. For example, if your co-worker has sent you an email asking for your opinion on a project, they don't expect a ten-page reply from you. They just want your thoughts at a high level. You should be able to send them this with a few minutes of your time.

The one-touch system has saved me countless hours and reduced my stress level immensely. Give it a try.

Become a Hard Thinker

Everyone talks about hard workers and—don't get me wrong—it is important to be a hard worker. However, I would like to suggest that is just as important to be a hard thinker. Hard workers focus on the project at hand, while hard thinkers first focus on more efficient and effective ways to get the project done or even if you should do the project at all.

Becoming a hard thinker requires that you look at the world a little differently and that you always:

- Question your assumptions. For example, using the goal of painting the shed that we discussed earlier, perhaps the shed really is very run down and should be replaced with a prefabricated shed from the local lumber yard.

3. Goal Setting

- Look for more efficient and effective ways to accomplish a task or project. Is there technology available that would help?
- Ask yourself whether a task or project should be done at all. Perhaps you no longer need a shed.
- Ask yourself if you know anyone with expertise who could provide input. Do you have the correct people on the team to get the project done?
- Question the timing of a project—does a delay help or hinder the project?
- Think, think, and think some more. You may save yourself time, effort, and money.

Samuel Goldwyn is given credit for the saying, "The harder I work, the luckier I get."

I suggest that we paraphrase this to read, "The harder I work and the harder I think, the luckier I get."

Other Ways to Achieve Your Goals

Here are a few more ideas that may help you achieve your personal and work-related goals:

- Peer pressure works. If you are working on a project, let your friends and family know. For example, when I told my family that I was writing a book, I felt some pressure to persevere and work to meet my goal.
- Reward yourself for achieving interim steps. This might be as simple as a glass of wine at the end of a day of productive work, or in my case, I get a sense of satisfaction from putting a happy face 😊 beside a completed step in my action plan.
- Celebrate successes with your team or family.
- Exercise to get the creative juices flowing. If you find that you are spinning your wheels and not making progress on a particular issue, go for a walk, bike, or run. You will often be surprised

- by the new ideas that come to you by just leaving the issue and coming back to it later.
- Focus on the key steps in your action plan. Remember that for most projects, 20% of the work gives you 80% of the results.

Summary

In this chapter, I have tried to illustrate goal setting and how to make an action plan through a few personal examples. As I said at the beginning of this chapter, goal setting and action plans go hand-in-hand—a goal without action is just a dream.

I also spent a good deal of time discussing SMART objectives. For most projects, your objective should be specific, measurable, attainable, realistic, and timeline focused. However, as illustrated in my "learning to play pickleball" example, there are times when the objective might be as vague as "learn and have fun." I've become a little more flexible in my old age.

I should also point out again that for most projects, your action plan should be accurate and absolutely focused on achieving your SMART objective efficiently and effectively. However, for some projects in which you are breaking new ground, this isn't possible. You simply don't know what you don't know, and as a result, your action plan will be iterative rather than linear. Once again, you will have to be flexible.

Perseverance and hard work, combined with careful thought, will overcome most obstacles. Perseverance is one of the most powerful attributes any person can have, but as I have constantly reiterated, life does also require you to think about your goals and the most effective and efficient way to achieve them.

Remember, life is not that complicated. You can accomplish almost any goal with an appropriate action plan.

Finally, reward yourself when you reach milestones and remember to have fun along the way.

Once again, you have homework: Pick a short-term goal (for example something that you can accomplish in a couple of weeks)

3. Goal Setting

and write down your action plan to achieve this goal as well as your reward once you have persevered and achieved this goal.

4. Finance

*"The goal isn't more money.
The goal is living your life on your terms."*
— CHRIS BROGAN

Why Is Understanding Your Finances Important?

For many people, if you mention the term "finance," their eyes glaze over and they quickly want to change the subject for fear that their perceived lack of knowledge will make them appear ignorant or foolish. To get started in the world of finance, all you really need to understand are a few basic terms and concepts. This chapter will help.

We all know what money is and how to spend it. This chapter is going to help you keep more of it. For me, that is what the focus of any discussion of finance should be about—keeping more of the money you make so that you improve your life and the lives of those you love.

The slow-and-steady investment growth system outlined in this chapter requires you to:

- determine how much discretionary income you have each month;
- save a set percentage of your discretionary income in a pension fund, TFSA, RRSP, or all three; and,

4. Finance

- watch your investments grow tax free with time and the magic of compound interest—remember, investing is a marathon not a sprint.

It is really not that complicated. Anyone can do it.

Financial Literacy

Finance, as with all subjects, has a few basic terms and concepts that you need to understand. Let's get started.

- *Gross income:* This is your income before the usual deductions, such as income tax, CPP, and so on that, for most of us, are deducted by our employer.
- *Net income:* This is the money you have coming in each month after deductions. For most of us, this comes from our job, after the usual deductions such as taxes, CPP, and so on.
- *Fixed expenses:* This is the money going out each month over which you have little control. Your fixed expenses would include money for food, rent or mortgage, utilities, and other items of a recurring nature that are a must-have.
- *Discretionary expenses:* These are the expenses that you have direct control over, such as dining out, new clothes, movie tickets, and so on. When you reduce your discretionary spending, you will find room for planning for your financial future. In order to get ahead financially, you must spend less than you earn. Consider this the first rule of finance.
- *Budgets:* Though difficult for most people, budgets do work. A budget is a summary of how you are going to spend your net income over a period of time, usually a month. In this chapter, I recommend that you have a broad-brush budget and you commit to saving a percent of your discretionary spending. For example, if you have a net income of $5,000 a month and fixed expenses of $4,000 a month that would leave you with $1,000 each month as discretionary spending. I recommend that you

save half ($500) in your pension at work, a RRSP or TFSA (see below). I also recommend that you do a thorough review of your discretionary spending with a view to reducing it and saving more.

- *Compound interest:* This is just interest on interest. For example, if you invested $1,000 at 10% interest payable annually, you would have $1,100 at the end of the first year ($1,000 plus 10% of $1,000), $1,210 at the end of the second year ($1,100 plus 10% of $1,100), and so on. Compound interest will make you wealthy. Albert Einstein said that compound interest is the greatest invention that the world has ever produced.

- *RRSP:* This is a registered retirement savings plan. This is a plan sanctioned by the government in which you get a tax break when you invest and your money grows tax free, but you must pay tax when you withdraw it. Compound interest works for you in a very big way. Appendix D in this chapter gives you a summary of the RRSP contribution rules.

- *TFSA:* This is a tax-free savings account. Again, this is a plan sanctioned by the Canadian government. No tax break when you invest, but it does grow tax free and there is no tax when you withdraw it. Since you can withdraw from a TFSA without paying any tax, it makes a great emergency fund. Note that once again, compound interest will work for you in a big way. Appendix C in this chapter gives you TFSA limits.

- *Defined benefit pension:* This is a type of pension in which your employer promises to pay a pension of a fixed amount based on a number of parameters such as age, years of service, and earning average. For example, your employer might pay 2% per year of service, based on the average salary of your last five years of service. Using specific numbers, if you have had thirty years of service and your average salary for the last five years is $50,000, then thirty multiplied by 2% is 60% and your pension would be 60% of $50,000 or $30,000 per year. Outside of government, very few of these plans are offered today.

- *Defined contribution pension:* This is a savings accumulation plan in which typically both you and your employer contribute. This fund grows tax free with the magic of compound interest. When you retire, you draw down this fund, but the money you withdraw is taxable.
- *Non-registered savings account:* This is an account you are using to save that is neither a RRSP nor a TFSA. You do not get a tax break and the money does not grow tax free, but the magic of compound interest is still available. This should usually only be used after you have reached the maximum allowed for your RRSP and TFSA.
- *MER:* This stands for management expense ratio. This is the fee you are charged by the investment firm to professionally manage your investments. For example, if you are paying $50 per year on a $10,000 balanced portfolio, the MER is 0.5%.
- *Balanced portfolio:* This is an investment that combines stocks and bonds often in a 50/50 ratio. The stocks provide the growth and the bonds provide security.
- *Exchange-traded funds (ETFs):* This is a type of investment that tracks a particular sector, industry, or stock market. For example, one ETF could simply track Canadian banks.

Growing Your Income

The first step to take on your financial journey is to consider how you can increase your monthly income. This is, of course, a very personal journey, but I have listed a few ideas below that may help you increase your income.

If you are an employee, ensure that you are being paid what you are worth. You may have to do some research and ask your boss for a raise, but this should be your first step on your financial plan. This step alone proved to be a huge bonus at least twice in my career when I declined an initial employment offer and held out for a better offer.

Consider monetizing a hobby where you have expertise. Photography is a good example.

Monetize your "genius." For example, if you have excellent people skills, perhaps you should be in sales.

Start a small business as a side hustle. The fastest way to becoming a millionaire is by owning your own business.

Slow-and-Steady Growth of Your Net Worth

Once you have tackled the income side of the financial equation, my slow-and-steady growth method involves saving a percentage of your discretionary spending, the power of time, and the magic of compound interest in either a defined contribution pension, RRSP, TFSA, or all three. Here are the steps involved:

1. Track your expenses over a period of a few months to determine which are fixed expenses and which are discretionary. Fixed expense include items such as:
    - rent or mortgage;
    - food;
    - utilities;
    - car payment;
    - Wi-Fi; and,
    - any items that you are committed to spend each month out of your control.
2. Subtract your fixed expenses from your net income to get your discretionary spending amount for a month. This is the money each month that you have complete control of and are often not sure how you manage to spend it all. For most people, this money is a black hole—money goes in your checking account but never comes out in the form of savings.
3. Commit to saving a fixed percent of your discretionary spending each month in a pension fund, RRSP, or TFSA. This is the pay-yourself-first system, but you are paying yourself from your discretionary spending total.

4. Finance

4. Work with a financial advisor, your financial institution, or a trusted friend or relative to set up both a TFSA and RRSP.

5. Keep in mind that the fees associated with these accounts (i.e., the MER) will slow your growth. The balance here for most investors is a question of comfort level. An investment advisor may charge a little more as a result of a higher MER, but you may sleep better at night knowing that they are in your corner. This is a personal decision, but as you become more comfortable, you will be able to manage more on your own.

6. Work with a financial advisor or an online system to automatically pay yourself the set percent from step three above. The management fees in your accounts should be low, and you should contribute to your pension, TFSA, and RRSP accounts first and then your non-registered accounts. If you are not comfortable doing this on your own, get help either from a financial advisor, your financial institution, or a trusted friend or member of your family. Remember, this is not rocket science. You are just setting up investment accounts into which you are going to automatically transfer money each month. Your investment advisor, bank/credit union, or trusted friend can help. You can do this!

Appendix C and Appendix D explain the rules involved for TFSAs and RRSPs. Later in this chapter, I illustrate both with a few examples.

The Magic of Compound Interest

Compound interest, as previously explained, is just interest on your interest. This means that not only are you getting interest on the principal amount invested, you are also getting interest on the interest that has been growing each financial period. In the scenarios below, you will see compound interest at its magical best.

Also, keep in mind that in a pension fund, TFSA, or RRSP, your money grows tax free. This is extremely important, as taxes would otherwise take a huge bite out of your saving. Both a RRSP and a TFSA are retirement saving tools but work almost opposite. A RRSP gives you a tax break when you invest, but you are taxed when you withdraw from it, and a TFSA allows you to withdraw tax free but no tax break when you invest. The magic of compound interest works equally well in both.

It is important to note that you cannot replicate the magic of compound interest by doing the math in your head. There is, of course, math involved but it becomes complex very quickly. Use an online site such as MyMoneyCoach.ca to verify the examples below for either your RRSP, TFSA, or pension fund, as they all grow tax free.

Scenario One

Assuming the following parameters, what would you guess that your retirement fund is worth at age sixty-five?

- Initial age that you begin investing: 40
- Principal amount when you begin investing at age 40: $0
- Monthly saving amount: $500
- Rate of return: 7%

And the answer is that at age sixty-five, the value of your investment will be $393,735.

You invested $150,000 (twenty-five years multiplied by twelve months per year multiplied by $500 per month), and the money grew to $393,735 with the magic of compound interest.

Scenario Two

Considering the same assumptions as above, you begin investing at age twenty rather than forty. In this case, the value of your investment at age sixty-five will be $1,778,832.

You invested $270,000 (forty-five years multiplied by twelve months per year multiplied by $500 per month) and your money grew to $1,778,832 with the magic of compound interest.

4. Finance

Just for interest sake, I've outlined the value of your investment at various ages below:

- Value of your investment at age 30: $86,000
- Value of your investment at age 40: $255,000
- Value of your investment at age 50: $588,000

Scenario Three

Considering the same assumptions as above, again, you begin investing at age twenty but invest $250 per month. In this case, the value of your investment at age sixty-five will be $889,416.

You invested $135,000 (forty-five years multiplied by twelve months per year multiplied by $250 per month) and your money grew to $889,416 through the magic of compound interest.

Scenario Four

The lesson in this scenario is that the fees you are charged to manage your investments make a huge difference.

Scenario four option one: You begin investing $250 a month at age twenty and earn 5% in a balanced fund. At age sixty-five, your investment is now worth $491,979.

Scenario four option two: Same parameters, but the fees associated with your balanced account are 2% less, and as a result, your return is 7% (5% plus 2% less in fees). In this option at age sixty-five, your investment is now worth $889,416.

Fees matter!

Stock Market Average Returns

The stock market can be very volatile. The average historical return has always been up, but it certainly has not been linear. There will be periods of significant decline in even well-managed balanced portfolios.

Also, keep in mind that over the long term, stocks beat bonds and bonds beat cash investments such as GICs.

In addition, you must account for inflation in calculating your real return. For example, if your portfolio increased in value 7% for the year and inflation was 2%, your real return is 5%.

The information below will give you an idea of the volatility of the Canadian TSX composite index excluding dividends:

- 2000: 1.7%
- 2005: 22.9%
- 2008: -35.5%
- 2009: 30.7%
- 2016: 17.5%
- 2018: -11.6%

This type of volatility can be nerve wracking, but keep in mind that the historical average is up. The TSX composite index average over the last thirty years has been up approximately 10% per year. Note again that this is the average over a thirty-year time period. The key is to stay invested over the long term and not panic in turbulent times.

Common Investment Mistakes

We all make mistakes, but the trick is to not only learn from your own mistakes, but also learn from the mistakes of others. Life is too short and there are far too many possible financial mistakes to make them all on your own. You have to also learn from the mistakes others have made in the past.

Here are a few of the most common ones for you to avoid:
- *Gambling rather than investing:* Hot stock tips from your friends or co-workers almost never work out in your favour. I gambled once in my career and it worked out, but I knew the company involved very well. However, when I repeated it for companies that I didn't know well, I lost money. The slow-and-steady

4. Finance

method outlined in this book will offer you a much better chance of success.

- *Not understanding the power of compound interest:* I have illustrated this concept in the previous scenarios. Go online and find a site to test a few scenarios of your own. A good site to try is MyMoneyCoach.ca.
- *Trying to time the market highs:* The stock market is not static—there are highs and lows, but over time, it does go up. Jumping in and out of the stock market to try to catch the highs and miss the lows is very difficult for experts and almost impossible for part-time amateur investors. Just stay the course. Over time, the market has always trended up.
- *Not understanding the impact of fees on the growth of your investment portfolio:* Scenario four above illustrates this point very well. The fees associated with your investments can significantly reduce your investment growth.
- *Not understanding the impact of taxes on your investment portfolio growth:* In this book, I recommend holding your investments in a pension fund, RRSP, or TFSA, where the investment grows tax free.
- *Not negotiating:* Keep in mind that almost everything financial is negotiable and that the profit on most investments is often made or lost at the point of purchase.
- *Not keeping track of your small purchases:* Small purchases are often the black hole that keep you broke and unable to invest in your future.
- *Other common investing mistakes include:*
    - not investing in a well-diversified portfolio;
    - believing that you can beat the stock market with your stock picks; and/or,
    - leaving retirement planning until later in your life.

The FIRE System—Financial Independence Retire Early

The FIRE (Financial Independence Retire Early) system is not a movement that I have followed, but it is worth mentioning in this chapter. Younger readers may find it interesting.

The FIRE system involves extreme frugality and saving up to 70% of your net income. The goal is to retire well before the more traditional retirement age of sixty-five. You then live off your savings. The investment recommendations of this chapter are still valid, but most of us don't have the discipline or desire to live as frugally as required to save up to 70% of our net income.

If you do a search on FIRE, you will find a great deal more information.

Our Financial Story

My wife and I are both retired. I worked for approximately forty-four years, primarily in the IT world, and my wife for approximately thirty years as a teacher. Both of us are receiving OAS and CPP. In addition, my wife has a defined benefit pension from teaching, and I am drawing down on a defined contribution pension plan. My defined contribution plan is primarily from a plan in which both my employer and I contributed 6% per year.

In addition, both of us have modest RRSPs and TFSAs.

When I was young, I didn't know what I know now. As a result, we didn't take full advantage of these tax advantaged investment opportunities. Life and lack of knowledge sometimes gets in the way.

We achieved our current financial position primarily as a result of:

- Living below our means. In other words, we spent less than we made.
- Investing in low-fee, tax-advantaged investments as outlined in this chapter.

- Buying assets that appreciated in value. Our home and cottage were our biggest investments. To be fair, almost any real estate investment of the '70s and '80s went up significantly in value.
- Reducing, as much as possible, our investments in assets that depreciated such as new vehicles. We drove used cars for most of our married life.
- Persevering on a slow and steady course.

We are living a very comfortable retirement, despite a few financial mistakes and missed opportunities. You don't have to get every investment decision 100% correct, and you don't need to worry about the small financial decisions. Just get the big ones right and have a long-term plan such as the one outlined in this chapter. This is somewhat contrary to the old adage "a penny saved is a penny earned." You don't want to waste money, but don't sweat the really small stuff.

What Would I Do Differently?

Financially, there are very few little things that I would do differently. The big change that I would've made is that early on in my IT career, I should have started my own business developing computer applications for local companies. I didn't realize it at the time, but in the early '70s, I had a unique set of skills that I could have leveraged. The message to you is that you too may have skills that you should take advantage of and grow your own company. There is risk, but the upside is huge. Most millionaires made their millions through their own business.

The second financial change that I would've made is that I would have bought farm land. Early in my career, I worked for a large agricultural company and, as a result, had a very large pool of agricultural expertise that I could have called on. Canadian farm land has increased exponentially in value.

Despite these errors of omission, my wife and I are enjoying a very comfortable retirement as a result of the steps outlined in this book.

Reducing Your Discretionary Spending

The key to the slow-and-steady investment growth system is finding additional ways to reduce your discretionary spending and saving your found money in low-fee, tax-advantaged portfolios. I have outlined below a few possible spending holes that you might consider plugging:

- *Interest charges:* If you have multiple debts at various rates, you should check with your financial institution to see if debt consolidation at a lower rate is possible. For example, if you have credit card debt, which is often over a 20% interest rate and a line of credit at your bank, which will be at a much lower interest rate, pay off the credit card with your line of credit.
- *Subscription charges:* Think of the online music, magazine, or newspaper subscriptions that you have and very seldom use. For most of us, this can easily be a few hundred dollars a year wasted.
- *Late payment charges:* Your credit cards and financial institution, for example, charge hefty fees. This is just wasted money.
- *Cable charges:* Are you paying for a service you don't need or perhaps channels that you never watch?
- *Cell phone:* Do you need all the bells and whistles and so on that you are being charged extra for?
- *Credit card impulse buying:* It has been proven that if you pay cash, you will buy less and, therefore, save more.
- *Insurance costs:* We all need home and auto insurance, but if you shop around for the best rates and raise your deductible, you will save hundreds each year.

These are just a few of the possible financial holes that you may be able to plug. Spend a few hours looking at your personal situation and you will find more. Be conscious of your spending habits.

4. Finance

How Long Will My Money Last?

A very common question people who have saved for retirement ask is how long their money is expected to last. There are numerous financial apps and websites that will give you an answer if you do a search on "how long will my money last?" I used a Cypress Credit Union site that I found by searching this way. This site asks you to enter four parameters: the amount of money you have to invest; the interest rate you are assuming for your investment growth; the monthly amount you need each month from your investments; and the expected annual inflation in percent (your monthly payment increases each year by this percent). I have a few scenarios outlined below.

Scenario One

Let's say:

- Starting balance of your investments: $400,000
- Expected rate of return on your investment: 5%
- Expected inflation rate: 2%
- Annual income you require from your investments: $25,000

In this case, your money is expected to last twenty-two years.

Scenario Two

Now, let's say:

- Starting balance of your investments: $1,000,000
- Expected rate of return on your investment: 4%
- Expected inflation rate: 2%
- Annual income you require from your investments: $40,000

In this case, your money is expected to last thirty-four years.

Try a few scenarios for yourself and keep in mind that in addition to the money that you are receiving from your investments, you and your significant other likely have other sources of income, such as OAS, CPP and possibly money from pensions and TFSAs.

Summary and Next Steps to Complete Your Financial Planning

The slow-and-steady method involves the following:

- Track your spending over a few months to determine your fixed expenses and how much discretionary income you have available.
- Set a goal of paying yourself first. This will be a percent of your discretionary income. This should be done with an automatic system as outlined in the step below. Don't trust yourself to do this on your own each month; it won't happen!
- Work with a financial advisor or an online system to automatically pay yourself the set percent from the second point above. The management fees in your accounts should be as low as you can negotiate. Your investments should be in your defined contribution pension, TFSA, and RRSP accounts first as they are tax advantaged. If you are not comfortable doing this on your own get help either from a financial advisor or a trusted friend or member of your family.
- Once you are comfortable with the low-fee accounts that you have set up, move your existing TFSA, RRSP assets into your low-fee index accounts. This may take a little time, but it is not complicated. You are just moving your money from one set of accounts with a high fee structure to your new accounts with a low-fee structure. Get help if you need it.
- Watch your money grow.
- Review your will or set up one up if you don't have one.
- Ensure that you have appropriate insurance.

4. Finance

📝 Your homework is to study the dos and don'ts outlined in Appendix B of this chapter and follow them as if your financial future was at stake—because it is!

Example One—Setting Up a TFSA

John is forty years old and has never had a TFSA. He does have a defined contribution pension through work into which both he and his employer contribute 5% of his income, but since he has only had this plan for a few years, John recognizes that this may not be sufficient to fund his retirement.

John recently inherited $100,000 and has decided to invest the bulk of this money in a TFSA and use the rest to make a one-time payment on his mortgage, which has a balance of approximately $300,000 at an interest rate of 5%. The terms of his mortgage allow for a one-time payment of 10% of the balance owing.

As a first step, John called the Canada Revenue Agency (CRA) TIPS line at 1-800-267-6999 to verify his TFSA contribution limit, which he learned was $63,500.

John then worked with his financial advisor to set up a low-fee, balanced TFSA for $63,500. He had also earlier determined that his discretionary income was approximately $1,500 per month and decided to further fund his TFSA with $500 per month starting in the new year.

John was also interested in calculating what his TFSA might grow to in twenty-five years. He used the site MyMoneyCoach.ca and set the parameters as follows:

- Initial amount invested: $63,500
- Term: 25 years
- Monthly amount invested: $500
- Rate of return: 5%

Using these parameters, in twenty-five years, John could have $509,000 for his retirement. Since the money is invested in a TFSA,

John can withdraw it tax free. Tax-free retirement money! How great is that!

Keep in mind, however, that John would not have received a tax deduction each year as Mary did with her RRSP contribution in the example below.

Example Two—Setting Up a RRSP

Mary is also forty years old and has also inherited $100,000. She has maxed out her TFSA, which has grown to approximately $110,000, but has no pension at work and has never had a RRSP.

Mary has decided to contribute all the $100,000 to a low-fee, balanced RRSP and to work with her current financial advisor, who has done an excellent job of growing her TFSA investments. Mary also has enough discretionary income to contribute $500 per month to her RRSP.

As a first step, Mary called the Canada Revenue Agency (CRA) TIPS line at 1-800-267-6999 to verify her RRSP contribution room. Since she does not have a work pension and has never contributed to a RRSP in the past and has the income to support it, Mary has enough RRSP contribution room for the entire $100,000, plus monthly contributions.

Mary then worked with her current financial advisor to set up a low-fee, balanced RRSP with an initial deposit of $100,000 and monthly recurring deposits of $500.

Mary also used the MyMoneyCoach.ca site to see what her RRSP might grow to using the following parameters:

- Initial amount invested: $100,000
- Term: 25 years
- Monthly amount invested: $500
- Rate of return: 5%

Using these parameters, in twenty-five years, Mary could have $632,000 for her retirement. This money is taxable when it is withdrawn, but Mary would have received a tax refund each year based

4. Finance

on her RRSP contributions. She could use this tax refund to fund her TFSA contribution, pay down debt, or, heaven forbid, spend it foolishly.

Example Three—Reducing Discretionary Spending

Joe and Beth take home approximately $6,000 per month between them but have nothing left at the end of the month and, in fact, have a $18,000 credit card debt with an interest rate of over 20%. Joe is forty-two and Beth is forty. Neither have a work pension or RRSPs or TFSAs. They plan to retire when Joe is sixty-five, but realize that if they continue on their current path, all they will have to live on in retirement is their OAS and CPP and any government supplemental income that they may qualify for. This is unacceptable, and as a result, they have decided to work with a financial advisor to review their financial situation and find opportunities to save for retirement.

Bob, their new advisor, recommends that as first step, they review their spending over the last six months. A summary is outlined below rounded to the nearest $50 for each category:

- Mortgage payment: $800
- Credit card debt: $500
- Home taxes: $400
- Utilities, including Wi-Fi, cell phones, electrical, cable, etc.: $500
- Eating out: $500
- Food and liquor: $1,500
- Clothing: $400
- Car payments: $700
- Car maintenance and gas: $400
- Home and vehicles insurance: $400
- Entertainment and sports: $250

- Medical/Pharmaceutical: $200
- Donations and gifts: $250
- Miscellaneous (can't be accounted for): $400

The grand total is $7,400 per month, so they are clearly living beyond their income and using their credit cards to subsidize their lifestyle.

Keep in mind that the above figures are an average over six months. Some months were much higher than $7,400, while some were slightly below $6,000, so clearly Joe and Beth can live within their means.

Bob, Joe, and Beth got to work and agreed to the following saving opportunities to reduce discretionary spending:

- Beth and Joe agreed to only use their credit cards for emergencies and only after talking the spending purpose over with each other. They plan to use cash for day-to-day purchases. This will reduce impulse spending.
- They have approximately $300,000 equity in their home and, as a result, were able to negotiate a line of credit at 5% interest. They then used the line of credit to pay off the credit card debt, which had an interest rate over 20%. In the short term, this will only save them $100/month, but in the long term, the savings will be significant.
- A summary of their monthly saving is outlined below:
    - Utilities (cancelled cable and found cheaper cell phone plans): $100
    - Saving from the second point above: $100
    - Eating out: $400
    - Food and liquor: $500
    - Clothing: $200
    - Insurance (higher deductible): $100
    - Entertainment: $100
    - Donations and gifts: $100
    - Miscellaneous (reduced impulse spending): $300

The $1,900 per month saving listed above reduces their average monthly expenses to $5,500 per month and leaves $500 per month

4. Finance

for retirement saving. Bob, their investment advisor, suggests they invest the $500 in TFSAs for the next twenty-three years until Joe's retirement. Assuming a 7% interest rate, they could have $333,000 of tax-free money in retirement.

In addition, Joe and Beth have only ten years left until their home is paid for. Also, both vehicles will be paid for in two years. These two expenses provide additional saving opportunities down the road. They have agreed to work with their investment advisor to set up RRSPs later.

Final Thoughts on Finance

Most millionaires earned their fortune by starting and running their own business, but I fully understand that not everyone wants or is capable of going down that path, so this book offers you an alternative slow-and-steady way to build your fortune. I also fully understand that many people find finance confusing and mind-numbingly boring. With this in mind, I have included a ten-point summary modified from the finance book *The Index Card: Why Personal Finance Doesn't Have to Be Complicated* by Helaine Olen and Harold Pollack (Olen and Pollack, 2016).

1. Maximize your RRSP, pension, and TFSAs since they all feature tax-free compound growth.
2. Buy inexpensive, well-diversified funds for the above (index funds not actively managed funds).
3. Never buy or sell an individual security and never invest in anything that you don't completely understand.
4. Save 20% of your money (see point one) and live below your means.
5. Pay credit card balances in full every month.
6. Buy appropriate life and asset insurance to reflect requirements at each point in your life.
7. Pay attention to fees and interest charges and be prepared to negotiate the price of everything major that you purchase.

8. Hire a financial advisor and ensure that they commit to the fiduciary standard.
9. Contribute monthly to charities of your choice.
10. Have an emergency fund; your TFSA can fit this role.

📝 Your homework is to make a copy of these ten points and put the copy in a place that ensures that you see it every day!

Resources You May Find Helpful

- Canada Revenue Agency (CRA): Canada.ca
- FIRE: financialindependenceretireearly.com
- Questrade: questrade.com
- MyMoneyCoach.ca
- MoneySense.ca
- Olen, Helaine, and H. Pollack. *The Index Card: Why Personal Finance Doesn't Have to Be Complicated.* London: Portfolio, 2016.
- TSX: money.tmx.com

Quotes You May Enjoy

I'll close this chapter with a couple of quotes that I like:

> *"I've been poor and I've been rich, rich is better."*
> — BEATRICE KAUFMAN

> *"The harder I work, the luckier I get."*
> — SAMUEL GOLDWYN

> *"An investment in knowledge pays the best interest."*
> — BENJAMIN FRANKLIN

4. Finance

"Opportunity is missed by most people because it is dressed in overalls and looks like work."
— THOMAS EDISON

*"I love money. I love everything about it.
I bought some pretty good stuff.
Got me a $300 pair of socks.
Got a fur sink. An electric dog polisher.
A gasoline powered turtleneck sweater.
And, of course, I bought some dumb stuff too."*
— STEVE MARTIN

Appendix B
Financial Dos, Don'ts, and Important Information

- Budgets don't work for many people, but you should know where you are spending your money, and a high-level budget will help. You will have fixed expenses and discretionary spending. The discretionary spending will be the source of your saving.
- Do pay yourself first and invest in a low-fee structure with diversified assets in a tax-free growth investment, such as your pension fund, RRSP, or TFSA. I recommend that you pay yourself a set percentage of your discretionary spending, and remember that the younger you start, the longer the magic of compound interest will work for you.
- Always pay credit card bill totals each month, never just the minimum. On a recent credit card statement with a $3,553 balance, my credit card company stated, in writing, that it would take thirty-one years and two months to pay off the balance if I made the minimum payment each month.
- Remember the Rule of 72. This rule tells you how long it takes for your investment to double with the magic of compound interest. Just divide the interest rate that you get into 72. For example, if you are earning 6% on an investment, it will double in twelve years (72 divided by 6). Go online and try a few

Appendix B   Financial Dos, Don'ts, and Important Information

examples to reinforce your understanding of compound interest. The site that I often use is MyMoneyCoach.ca.
- Keep in mind that the fees reduce your investment growth.
- Spend less than you make is the first rule of financial growth.
- Do all that you can to legally minimize the tax you pay.
- Note that financial risk comes in many forms: market risk, inflation risk, pandemic risk, lack of knowledge risk, and so on. Do your homework.
- When you sell your principal residence, the money is tax free.
- Monitor your financial progress regularly.
- Don't sweat the small financial transactions. Just get the big financial decisions right. As long as you are spending less than you make and saving a significant portion of the difference, you will be fine in the long run.
- Do your homework and trust your judgment. If you don't fully understand an investment, walk away from it.
- If your employer offers a voluntary contribution pension plan in which your employer will match your contribution, then you should contribute the maximum allowed. The employer contribution is free money.
- As you get closer to retirement, you should reduce or eliminate debt.
- Don't pay too much for guarantees. A classic example is a reverse mortgage for seniors. In a reverse mortgage, the financial company agrees to pay you a certain amount each month based on the equity that you have in your home. Since the financial company is paying you, hence the term "reverse mortgage." In most cases, you will be much better off to obtain a line of credit.
- The concept of annuities are beyond the scope of this chapter. Get expert, unbiased advice if you are considering an annuity.
- Don't think that you can beat the financial experts. Get help either from a financial advisor or an online system that handles your investments for you. You don't know what you don't know,

and I guarantee that over 90% of people will not beat the experts. Do yourself a favour and play the odds.
- Whenever possible, buy assets that appreciate in value and not assets that depreciate. Vehicles are the big exception, but used vehicles depreciate slower.
- Remember that as you grow older, your investments should be more conservative.
- Use an automated payment of bills whenever possible. This will make your life simpler and eliminate late payment or interest charges.
- Avoid all interest payments. Home mortgage and car payments are the big exceptions.
- Remember that a bargain is only a bargain if you like and use what you buy. Look at the clothes or shoes in your closet that you never wear and that universal gym in the basement.
- Ensure that you have appropriate insurance, both life and loss of income insurance, for the various stages of your life. An insurance professional can help.

Appendix C
TFSA Contribution Limits

TFSAs have been around since 2009. The yearly limits are outlined below:

- 2009–2012: $5,000
- 2013–2014: $5,500
- 2015: $10,000
- 2016–2018: $5,500
- 2019–2022: $6,000

Your contribution total for above period of time is $69,500. Therefore, if you have never had a TFSA, you can contribute the maximum. However, keep in mind that each tax year you are allowed the contribution limit for that year as an additional contribution to your TFSA total.

The contribution limit for the TFSA is indexed to inflation for future years and rounded to the nearest $500.

If you have questions about your personal TFSA information, call CRA TIPS at 1-800-267-6999. You will need your SIN and information on your recent tax return to verify your identity.

Appendix D
RRSP Contribution Rules

A registered retirement savings plan (RRSP) is a retirement savings plan for Canadians. In a RRSP, your money compounds tax free and you get a tax deduction for the amount of deposit in the tax year of reckoning. However, unlike a TFSA, you must pay tax when you withdraw funds. The logic behind the RRSP tax thinking is that when you withdraw the money, you will be retired and, therefore, in a lower tax bracket than when you were working.

RRSP rules are somewhat complex. I am only going to review the highlights here.

The first topic to understand is the contribution deduction limit for each tax year. These are outlined below for the last three years:

- 2020: $27,300
- 2019: $26,500
- 2018: $26,230

Your deduction limit for any given year is also limited by the lesser of the limit for the year or 18% of earned income in that year. For example, if you earned $100,000 in 2020, your deduction limit would be 18% of $100,000 or $18,000 since this is less than $27,300. This amount would be further reduced by any pension or deferred profit-sharing plan you or your employer made on your behalf. Therefore, the RRSP contribution limit of $27,300 for the 2020 tax year is reduced by:

Appendix D   RRSP Contribution Rules

- the 18% of income rule; and,
- pension or profit-sharing contributions.

The good news is that your contribution limit is the total of your unused RRSP deductions from previous years. If you don't use your RRSP deduction in any given year, you don't lose it. Your contribution limit grows, but you are losing out on the magic of compound interest for these unused contribution years. Also, keep in mind that the last year that you can make a RRSP contribution is the year you turn seventy-one.

The following is a simple example:

John made $100,000 pre-tax income in 2019. He has no pension plan; therefore, he could contribute 18% of $100,000 ($18,000) or $26,500, whichever is less to his RRSP. John decides to make a $10,000 RRSP contribution for 2019. This leaves $8,000 RRSP contribution room for future years.

If you are unsure of your RRSP contribution limit, you can check your last notice of assessment or call the CRA TIPS line at 1-800-267-6999.

5. Health and Wellness

*"Your body is your most priceless possession;
you've got to take care of it."*
— JACK LALANE

Why Should Health and Wellness Be a Priority?

Health and wellness has always been a topic of interest for me, but as a result of a traumatic period in my life, health and wellness is now a priority. Here is my story.

For the first fifty years of my life, I was really very healthy, despite having paid very little attention to my diet, my exercise program, how much sleep I got, or the stress in my life. This caught up to me around the time I turned fifty.

As stated earlier, I worked most of my life for a large IT company. It was, and is, an excellent but very demanding organization. The hours were long and the standards were high. In the late '90s, certification became the buzzword of the day in this company and most staff were required to certify in one or more of the company's recognized professions. As it happened, the profession that I worked in required me to first certify in another profession prior to being eligible to certify in the profession that I currently worked in. I chose project management (PM) as the initial profession that I would certify in. The process to

5. Health and Wellness

certify in PM for my company involved the following: applying to an external body (Project Management Institute; PMI) with a resume and an academic transcript in order to obtain permission to write an online standard test based on PM knowledge; passing the test with a mark of at least 70%; submitting a mini thesis to my own company; flying to a central interview location to be interviewed by three different PM professionals on the information in my mini thesis; and receiving a pass by at least two of the three interviewers. If I was able to get through all of this, I could then start on the certification process for the profession that I actually worked in. This, combined with my normal business workload and the usual life and family issues, finally was too much.

I am giving you this background so that you can understand the stress that I was under and appreciate that a breakdown was coming. I became very depressed and was looking for any excuse to end it all. For example, when I was about to write the online PMI exam, my excuse to end the suffering was not getting at least 80%, as I had learned that for people in my company, 80% was the unwritten standard, not 70% required by PMI. Fortunately, I passed with a mark higher than 80% and was able to navigate through the rest of the two certification processes, but the depression remained and I continued to struggle with life.

My wife was very understanding and finally convinced me that I had to get help. Keep in mind that when you are mentally ill, you are not thinking clearly. It hadn't occurred to me that help might be available. I went to a doctor and began taking medication for depression, but it took at least another six months before I was even close to normal, and the medication led to another problem, which I will discuss next.

After several months on the medication for depression, I began to have occasional seizures at night. At the time, we didn't know that I was having seizures, as it was dark and all my wife knew was that I would thrash about in bed and make odd noises. It was a strange experience, but we didn't give it much thought until I had a seizure during the day and my wife could see what was happening to me. She was a teacher for close to thirty years and had students with epilepsy, so she knew what a seizure looked like. The seizures progressed from being exclusively at night to occasionally during the day, and as a result, I lost my licence to drive for a year. I went through a great many tests and saw several medical professionals. Ironically, after a great deal of research, we determined that the seizures were caused by the medication that I was taking for depression.

I am giving you this background to understand that I have been through a serious mental health issue, which then caused a serious physical health issue. As a result, I have given health and wellness a great deal of thought. I was forced to make significant changes to my lifestyle and I now know what works for me, and I sincerely hope that my recommendations will work for you.

Know Your Own Health First

Prior to making any changes in your life, I strongly recommend that you have a complete physical with a physician that you trust. It is imperative that you have a full understanding of any underlying health issues that you may have prior to changing your physical and mental lifestyle.

If you smoke, I also strongly urge you to quit now. Smoking will take years off your life, as will excessive drinking. Help is available. Take advantage of all the programs available.

I also recommend that you, in consultation with your doctor, ensure that all your immunizations are current. I know that some of you are thinking that this is a strange request, however, this is important; the COVID-19 vaccination raised this issue for me in 2021. Immunization works, and I don't just mean getting your flu shot each year, your COVID shot, or just your childhood vaccinations. You should talk this over with your doctor and should also consider other vaccinations, such as those for shingles if you have had chicken pox, pneumonia, and any others recommended by your doctor. Vaccinations work and are very low risk. Why would you risk a serious health issue that a simple vaccination can prevent?

You should also consider having a genetic health test. There are many on the market today, and while my wife and I have not taken

5. Health and Wellness

this step yet, we are going to in the near future, as we have had a genetic issue brought to light in our immediate family. This issue isn't very likely to be life threatening, but it is a mutation that may have been inherited from one of us. This mutation involves abnormal blood clotting and may be important to know about if we need surgery. Forewarned is forearmed.

My final recommendation is that you be prepared to research any health issues that you may have. The internet is an excellent source of reliable information, and no one is more interested in your health than you and your family are. You need to be an advocate for yourself and your family. Your doctor likely sees hundreds of patients with countless ailments and can't possibly be an expert on all of them. Do your own digging. An anecdotal example is the issue that I had with seizures. It took a great deal of research on my part to determine that the seizures were likely caused by the anti-depression medication that I was on.

The Seven Key Ingredients to Health and Wellness

After years of researching and experimenting with what works for me, I found that if I was struggling mentally or physically, I could narrow it down to a problem with one or more of the following seven key areas:

1. Nutrition
2. Exercise
3. Sleep and rest
4. Social interaction
5. Mental health
6. Sense of purpose
7. Balance

I'll discuss each of these in more detail below, but keep in mind that this chapter isn't a clinical study on mental and physical health. This is what works for me. You will have to think about your personal situation and determine what works for you, but it is my sincere hope that my story will help you.

Nutrition

If I am struggling mentally or physically, I look first to diet, exercise, and sleep to get myself back on track. I am, therefore, going to review these topics first.

There have been countless books written on nutrition and diet. My approach is really very simple and based on the Canada food guide, which recommends the following:

- Eat plenty of fruits and vegetables.
- Protein is required but limit your intake of red meat.
- Choose whole grains and avoid food with additives and preservatives.
- Water should be your drink of choice, but tea or coffee in moderation are fine; however, drinks high in sugar are not.

I know that many of you are thinking that it can't be that simple. It is, but here are a few more guidelines:

- Watch your calorie intake and balance your diet to your exercise program. I am a big believer in the calories in/calories out equation in order to keep your weight under control. Weigh yourself regularly and consider keeping a journal or spreadsheet to track fluctuations in your weight.
- Work with your doctor to determine a healthy weight and work towards it. Remember, obesity kills.
- Avoid snacks, but if you do snack, snack healthy and try not to eat between your evening meal and breakfast.
- Whenever possible, avoid eating highly processed food or foods with preservatives, artificial colours, or other additives. For example, I determined that I can tolerate a small amount of MSG but will have a very violent reaction if the MSG content is higher, and as a result, I avoid all food with an MSG additive.

- Take a multi-vitamin every day.
- Drink alcohol only in moderation.

Diet is really this simple. Moderation, discipline, and balance are key, and developing the habit is vital, so make it easy to follow these habits:

- Keep healthy snacks on hand.
- Make a list when you shop and include lots of fruit and vegetables.
- Don't buy junk food or sugary drinks, except for special occasions.
- Limit fast food to about once a month.
- Leave yourself a note about eating healthy on the fridge and pantry doors.
- Take whatever steps you need to take to develop eat healthy eating habits.

Think about what you put into your body and remember that healthy eating is just a habit that you can develop.

Exercise

We have all seen and read articles on the benefits of exercise, but the most remarkable statistics involve exercise and longevity. The World Health Organization (WHO) recommends 150 minutes of moderate activity or 75 minutes of vigorous activity each week. The results of a study on exercise by the WHO found that:

- those who exercised a little but did not meet the WHO standards lowered their risk of premature death by 20%;
- those who met the WHO standard of moderate exercise reduced their risk of early death by 31%; and,
- those who tripled the recommended standard by simply walking for 450 minutes per week reduced their risk of premature death by 39%.

An exercise program is just another habit that you can develop in the same way that you develop the habit of eating healthy.

I exercise ten to fifteen hours a week. My exercise program involves:
- Walking;
- Biking;
- golfing (if I spend four hours golfing, I count two hours as exercise and I always walk);
- playing pickleball; and,
- strength and flexibility training three or four times a week for an hour,

I'm retired and, as a result, have more time for exercise. When I was working, I didn't average more than three or four hours a week, but I did get some exercise each week despite the pressures of work and family.

In order to develop a serious exercise habit when I retired, I took the following steps that may work for you to help you get started:

1. I kept a log of my exercise program. When I first started the log, it was on paper, and later, I kept a spreadsheet. I no longer keep a log, as my exercise habit is now just part of my life.
2. I joined a gym near home and walked to the gym three or four times a week.
3. I put studded tires on my bike so that I could bike year-round. I have bad knees, so running is not an option, but biking works for me. Swimming could also be an option for those with bad joints.
4. When all the gyms closed because of the pandemic, I bought some exercise bands and continued strength and flexibility training at home.

In short, I did whatever I could to make getting exercise easy. Remember, just going for a walk will make you feel better and may extend your life. You don't need an expensive gym in your basement! Exercising is just another habit, but it's one that may extend your life.

5. Health and Wellness

Finally, a word of caution: The first thing that you should do is see your doctor and have a complete physical to ensure that you are healthy enough to start a new exercise program. If you are significantly overweight or have an underlying health condition, you may also want to work with a personal trainer.

Sleep and Rest

Doctor Felix Veloso, in his book *Healthy Aging Naturally: Proven Strategies for Disability-Free Longevity* (Veloso, 2020), outlines several impacts of sleep including the following:

- *Longevity:* Regularly sleeping less than six to eight hours a night increases your chance of early death by 12%.
- *Obesity:* Sleep deprivation is associated with obesity
- *Weakened immunity:* Sleep moderates and maintains the immune system and sleep deprivation weakens your immunity to viral and bacterial infections.
- *Learning and memory:* Sleep before and after studying enhances learning and long-term memory.
- *Creativity:* REM sleep enhances creative problem solving.
- *Brain detoxification:* Natural sleep aids in the elimination of neurotoxic garbage, particularly beta-amyloid, which is associated with Alzheimer's disease.
- *Depression:* Insomnia engenders psychiatric disorders, particularly depression.

I think that you get the message—healthy sleep habits are critically important to your overall health.

Social Interaction

I have often described myself as a "lone wolf." I'm quite happy even when my social contacts are limited to my wife and immediate family. I don't feel a need to have people in my life to socialize with on a regular basis. Even when I exercise, I prefer to, for example, walk or bike on my own or with my wife. My wife, however, is very social and, given a choice, always picks group workout programs over individual ones. Needless to say, the pandemic has been easier for me to cope with than it has for my wife and countless others.

The point here is that we all have a need for social interaction, but for some their "social net" is quite wide, while others, like me, need few regular social contacts. My evidence to support that this seems to be a genetic trait is mostly anecdotal evidence: the Schmalenberg family has a great many lone wolves going back as far as I can recall, including my father and my paternal grandfather. One niece even remarked, only half jokingly, that the Schmalenberg family is made for pandemics since we don't have any problems with isolating.

Because my evidence that sociability is influenced by our genetic makeup is anecdotal, I decided to do a little research. It turns out that genetics do play a significant role. In his article "The Sociability Spectrum: Evidence from Genetics" (2020), Christopher Badcock, PhD, states that "clearly, there is more to genetics of sociability than meets the eye."

For many years, I felt guilty about the fact that I wasn't really a very social person, but I have finally accepted the fact that it is just the way I am, and it's OK. I try to be more flexible with my wife's need for more social interaction, and she has accepted the fact that I'm very much a lone wolf. Compromise has been required.

The key point of this discussion is that we all have sociability needs to varying degrees and that there is evidence that our genetic makeup influences our sociability. Accept who you are, but be prepared to compromise with those you love who may have different sociability requirements.

Mental Health

Your mental health requires the same care and attention as your physical health. Unfortunately, I figured this out the hard way and, as a result, had a serious mental breakdown. Since then, I have paid far

5. Health and Wellness

more attention to how I am feeling mentally, and if I am struggling, I take steps to get myself back on track, including the following:

1. Confiding In a Trusted Person

After years of keeping things to myself, I found that talking problems over with my wife helped me see things more clearly and put things in perspective. My wife has excellent judgement and knows me better than I know myself.

Find someone whom you can confide in. From personal experience, I know that it helps.

2. Checking the Physical Issues in My Life

Very often, if I am struggling mentally, it's because I'm struggling physically as well. I walk a very narrow path when it comes to sleep, nutrition, and exercise. If I stray too far from my narrow norms, I risk a depression episode.

For many people, keeping a journal helps, as you can then look back and will often see where you went off track. As an aside, journals work for many different purposes.

3. Not Repeating the Same Mistakes

As I stated earlier, my father often said that life is just too short to just learn from your own mistakes; you have to learn from the mistakes of others as well, or you will be doomed to a life of mistakes.

Often our repeated mistakes are a result of bad habits. For example, being chronically late is nothing more than a bad habit that as a result adds stress and anxiety to your life and to those who depend on you. Similarly, exercise and nutrition are habits that you can develop. Stopping at a fast food restaurant after your workout at the gym is just a bad habit that can be broken.

4. Not Dwelling On the Past

We have all done the "woulda, coulda, shoulda" review of events of the past that we believe didn't unfold as we wanted. This is fine as a learning exercise for similar events of the future, but when we rehearse the events over and over, losing sleep and productive time in the present, it is time to let it go.

I've found that if I am dwelling on an old issue, documenting the problem helps. This can be as simple as stating the problem in a few sentences, along with an outline of the new solution. This simple act helps me let it go and reinforces the learning.

I also talk it over with my wife; she has amazing judgment and insight.

5. Not Focusing on Things Out of My Control

Focusing on issues out of my control is an area that I sometimes struggle with. For example, I follow the stock market very closely, and one day, I was moaning and groaning that the market was going down and my retirement investments were suffering. I was on the golf course at the time, and my golf partner put things in perspective by asking if that meant my money was now only going to last until I was 115 years old rather than 120—I got the message.

The current pandemic is another example of an issue out of our control, but there are steps that we can take to mitigate the risk. This is true of most problems. Just document the issue and the mitigation steps that you are going to take and move on.

6. Letting Poisonous People into My Life

I have only met two people in my life who were really and truly people that I did not want to associate with, but we have all met a few with character flaws that can negatively influence your life. For example:

- chronic complainers;

5. Health and Wellness

- those who only see the negative in everything;
- people who are always putting others, including you, down; and,
- racists, sexists, and homophobic people.

You become a composite of those you associate closely with, so be vigilant. Not every friend or associate is worth keeping. Sometimes, the price is too high in terms of your mental health.

Finally, another word of caution. Remember that help is available if you are struggling mentally. Listen to those close to you and follow up if they suggest that you need help.

7. Mental Stimulation

When I first retired, I was quite content to read, golf, exercise, watch TV, and spend time with my family. After a few years, this was no longer enough. In simple terms, I was bored.

I had an idea for this book percolating in my mind for several years but simply hadn't the courage to tackle it. Fear of failure was the biggest impediment. I had no experience with writing a book and getting it published, so for the first few months, I didn't tell anyone but my wife and daughter. I guess I thought that if I found it too hard, I could just drop the book idea and very few people would know of my failure. This worked for a couple of months, but not for long. At a family gathering my two sons asked me if I had anything to tell them and I had to come clean. Everyone was very supportive, but I have to admit, I still feel the pressure of tackling something that is completely outside my comfort zone. However, I now know the mental stimulation of writing is great for my sense of well-being.

For the first few weeks, I felt guilty if I didn't write for four or five hours a day, but then I became more realistic and aimed for ten to fifteen hours a week. This had provided me with the mental stimulation I need, without the pressure of what previously felt like a job.

Clearly, writing a book isn't for everyone, but we all need a regular challenge and mental growth. For most people, their career provides the mental challenge that they need. I know that it certainly did for me, but even when I was working, I had hobbies that took a few hours a week and provided a break from my day-to-day job. The key is to find hobbies that really interest you and that you can work into your life without neglecting family obligations. Life balance is key—see below.

Sense of Purpose

According to Anthony L. Burrow from Human Development at the Cornell College of Human Ecology, in the article "The Benefits of Having a Sense of Purpose" (Jackie, 2022), a sense of purpose is integral to the human experience and how we relate to the world. He says it is not just a goal, but "an intention to do something in the world" and it helps us stay stable. Find something to look forward to, such as volunteering at charity or non-profit organization. Helping others is a good way to feel purpose, as sense that you are making the world a better place.

Balance

Balance in your life is about being content with the decisions that you are making for all areas of your life: family, work, social, sense of purpose, physical activity, and so on. Balance involves setting priorities and making choices to keep those areas of your life that are important to you and letting go of things that are not a priority.

Balance means taking care of yourself physically through nutrition, rest, and exercise. It also involves taking care of yourself mentally by setting boundaries and priorities. Without boundaries and priorities, you will be constantly stressed by countless conflicting demands for your time. You will have to learn to say no if you want your boundaries and priorities respected.

Balance in your life is a journey with constant ups and downs as your circumstances change. It requires you to continually examine your priorities, but keep in mind that setting priorities will reduce your stress levels and make you more productive.

A good example for me personally is the boundary that I have set regarding being a handy man. When we were young and broke, I tackled all sorts of do-it-yourself projects but really did not enjoy it. Being a do-it-yourself person caused me a great deal of stress. After many years, I recognized this boundary. Now my favourite tool is the telephone: I call the professionals to get the job done.

Summary

I sincerely hope that while reading this chapter on health and wellness, you said to yourself, "Wow, this stuff really isn't all that complicated. I can do this!"

Most of what I have discussed in this chapter is nothing more involved than developing a few new habits in the seven key areas that I consider to be essential to health and wellness. Focusing on those seven areas has worked for me, and I believe that it will work for you too. This is a classic example of Occam's Razor: simple obvious steps are usually the correct course of action.

Your homework is to diligently follow the seven steps below:

1. *Nutrition:* Look up the Canada food guide and follow it.
2. *Exercise:* Start by walking for half an hour a day and track your progress in a journal. Walking, running, or biking are cheap and easy to do almost any time or place.
3. *Sleep and rest:* Start with eight hours of sleep a night and at least one day of rest a week. Adjust from there based on how well you are coping.
4. *Social interaction:* Accept who you are but be prepared to compromise.
5. *Mental health:* Confide with someone you trust and be prepared to seek help. Consider keeping a journal to help you pinpoint where you have problems.

6. *Sense of purpose:* Volunteering at a charity might be a good option. Writing this book has given me a sense of purpose during the covid pandemic.
7. *Balance:* Recognize the boundaries that you have set in your life, but ensure that you and those important to you are healthy and happy.

Make the seven key ingredients to health and wellness work for you. This is not complicated!

Suggested Reading

- Babcock, Christopher. "The Sociability Spectrum: Evidence from Genetics," *Psychology Today.* Posted June 27, 2020. https://www.psychologytoday.com/intl/blog/the-imprinted-brain/202006/the-sociability-spectrum-evidence-genetics.
- Morin, Amy. *13 Things Mentally Strong People Don't Do: Take Back Your Power, Embrace Change, Face Your Fears, and Train Your Brain for Happiness and Success.* New York: William Morrow Paperbacks, 2017.
- Swift, Jackie. "The Benefits of Having a Sense of Purpose," Cornell Research. Last modified November 7, 2022. https://research.cornell.edu/news-features/benefits-having-sense-purpose.
- Veloso, Felix. *Healthy Aging Naturally: Proven Strategies for Disability-Free Longevity.* Regina: Your Nickel's Worth Publishing, 2020.

6. Productivity

"The main thing is to keep the main thing the main thing."
— STEPHEN R. COVEY

Why Is Being Productive So Important?

I love the above quote from Stephen Covey about "keeping the main thing the main thing," because it has been my experience that there are many situations that illustrate how often we get distracted from our priorities. For example, let's say that one Saturday morning, you decide to clean out and organize the junk in your shed, only to find that the tire of one of the bikes in the shed needs air, so you pump the tire up and then go for a bike ride instead of cleaning the shed. We have all done something like this in the past, and while we may have regretted it later, no real harm was done. However, how about the time you sat down with your recent tax returns and your computer to do some retirement planning and found yourself playing solitaire on your computer instead. Two years later, and you still have no idea about your retirement situation—this might come back to haunt you.

Productivity can be defined as "doing the right things right." This combines effectiveness (doing the right things) with efficiency (doing it right). For example, let's assume that your checking account is overdrawn and the bank manager has called you about it and wants you to correct it immediately. The most effective and efficient way to fix this is for you to sit down at your computer for a few minutes and transfer money to your checking account from your savings account. I've known people to resolve this situation by going to the bank and taking out a loan to cover the overdraft, which takes hours, not minutes, and they ended up with money drawing no interest in their savings account. Their solution was neither effective nor efficient, and while there may be good reasons for not touching the money in their savings account, they now have a loan to pay back.

In keeping with the theme of this book, whenever you are faced with a challenge, sit down and think for a few minutes about the most effective and efficient way to resolve the problem. Thinking through your options will often save you time and money and make you more productive.

Focus on Your Priorities

Look at the following list of sayings that we commonly use about our priorities:
- "Get your priorities straight."
- "First things first."
- "The urgent shouldn't supersede the important."
- "It's not a priority."
- "Keep the main thing the main thing."

The key point to remember is that you must give your priorities the status that they deserve and focus on the job at hand. Doing this one thing well will immediately make you more productive. Don't spend your life working on the trivial and neglecting the important. In other words, don't confuse activity with productivity.

Your Habits Are Key

I've dedicated an entire chapter of this book to habits because your habits are also the key to your productivity and, ultimately, the key to your success in all areas of your life, including your health, your relationships, and your finances. Remember, successful people are simply people with successful habits.

I know that I am beginning to sound like a broken record with all this talk about habits, but habits really are extremely important—so important that they warrant homework.

📝 Your homework is to take half an hour and list following:
- One bad habit that you want to eliminate. Don't pick something hard, such as quitting smoking. Start with something much smaller, such as not hitting the snooze button over and over in the morning, which results in you starting the day late and rushed.
- One positive new habit that you are going to develop. Again, I suggest that you pick something simple, such as starting each day by creating a to-do list for the day and resolving to diligently follow it.

If you are struggling with this assignment, go back and read the chapter on successful habits again.

Occam's Razor

As stated earlier, Occam's razor is a heuristic, or rule of thumb, that states that whenever you are faced with multiple explanations for a problem or situation, the simplest one is likely the correct one.

William of Occam is given credit for this rule of thumb. He stated that the best explanation for any phenomenon is the one that makes the fewest assumptions. A statement that includes, for example, many assumptions should be questioned using Occam's razor. For example, how likely is it that all the governments of the world and the medical and scientific experts got together and agreed to create the COVID-19 pandemic? Isn't it far more likely that there really is a COVID pandemic that has killed millions?

A metaphor associated with Occam's razor states that if you hear hoof beats, think horses, not zebras. It's been my experience that many people think zebras when the answer is far simpler.

If the simplest explanation is usually the correct one, we can use this principle to become more productive. For example, if you are trying to lose weight, exercise more and eat less junk food might be a good start. If you are planning for retirement, spend less and save more seems like a possible simple solution.

Occam's razor won't always work, but it's a good starting point for any problem.

Productivity Habits and Tools

I have several productivity tools and habits that help me organize my life. These include:

- *To-do lists:* A to-do list organizes and sets priorities for your day and should leave you with a sense of accomplishment, not a feeling of defeat, so challenge yourself with your to-do list, but don't overwhelm yourself.
- *One-touch system:* Handle some action items with one iteration rather than spend so long thinking about it that you do not complete the task. Action items that seem to hang around are a terrible stress creator. Don't let this happen to you.
- *Being proactive:* Proactive people set goals and move projects forward. For some, this is a natural skill, but for most of us, proactivity can be learned and enhanced with practice. Review Chapter 3 on setting and achieving goals to help you become more proactive.
- *Goal setting and action plans:* Again, review Chapter 3 on goal setting and action plans, as this is another key to becoming more productive. The three main ingredients involved in achieving your goals involve nothing more than:
    - SMART objectives;
    - action plans; and,

- working your action plans and persevering, persevering, and persevering some more.

Key Priorities

Let's take a few minutes and look at what should be the most important priorities in most peoples lives. For example, would you list the following priorities in the same order as I have them listed?

1. Your significant other and your family
2. Your health
3. Balance and meaning in your life including your career
4. Your faith
5. Your finances

You may not have listed the above priorities in the same order as I have, but for most people, these would at least be at or near the top of their life priority list.

The next question to ask is, are you living your life in alignment with your priorities? If you are not, then it's time to make a few changes since, for example, your financial situation should not be a higher priority than your family.

Build on Your Strengths

When I was young, the common theme in education was overcoming your weaknesses in order to be successful. Over the years, I have concluded that this is wrong. Your strengths are the keys to your success, and you only need to overcome those weaknesses that will significantly impede your strengths. Don't let your weaknesses control your life.

For example, I have very poor fine-motor skills and I am not at all artistic. As a result, my art work was atrocious, and though my hand writing is legible, it's not up to most teacher's standards. This caused some issues for me in elementary school, but no matter how often I practised my hand writing, it was marginal at best. Computers are a blessing for people like me since I can now type almost everything and the reader can now focus on the message and not the medium.

Whatever success I have had I attribute primarily to my strengths, which include my ability to:

- focus on achieving the goals that I set;
- maintain good habits;
- understand basic financial principles, such as compound interest;
- focus on the key issues in problems that I encountered; and,
- work with a team of amazing people, including, most significantly, my wife.

Now take a few minutes to think about some of the very successful people in your life. I think that you will find that they too focused on a small number of strengths, such as:

- the amazing teacher who had an uncanny ability with children;
- the doctor with the calming bedside manner;
- the farmer who always seemed to be more successful than his neighbours; and,
- the carpenter who completed every project on time and on budget and always had happy clients.

These people focused on their strengths and, as a result, were very successful and had less stress in their life because they simply got help in improving the weaker areas of their life. A simple quote to remember is that you should "bet on your strengths and hire your weaknesses."

Get Help from Good People

When you focus on your strengths, that also means that you must understand what your weaknesses are and get help when you need it. This sounds very easy, but most of us are reluctant to ask for help and it often isn't obvious who in our life is in the best position to help. What I am saying is that asking for help from the right people is, in itself, an amazing skill that will make you more productive. This isn't a skill that you should take lightly. Get to know the people in your home and work life and their key strengths.

I can think of one situation in my business life where I was in over my head on a project. This project involved negotiating and creating a very large contract involving hundreds of millions of dollars. I had never done anything like this before, and as a result, the negotiations dragged on for many months. Fortunately, my boss realized that I needed help, and we finally completed the negotiations and signed the contract. In this case, my reluctance to ask for help could have been disastrous. It was a little hard on my ego to have help parachuted in, but it was the correct decision.

A follow-up to getting help from good people is avoiding or removing poisonous people from your life. Fortunately, poisonous people are rare, but we have all met a few and probably let them influence our life longer than we should have.

If you work for an organization where people take coffee breaks together, one example of a step that you can take involves who you go for coffee with. Pick the successful, positive people.

Remember, we become a composite of the people we let in our life. Removing poisonous people from your life may seem harsh, but keep in mind that people very seldom change and this is often the only answer to a difficult situation. Don't let poisonous people poison you.

Persistent Action

Successful people are, almost without exception, very persistent, and so they are more productive because they persist until they achieve their goals. I'm sure that these people were not born this way. Persistence and perseverance are likely learned behaviours. I'm almost sure there are no persistence and perseverance genes.

The key questions then become: How do you become more persistent and perseverant? Are there habits that you can develop? As I'm sure you've guessed, there are habits that help, including the following:
- Simple to-do lists—just the act of writing a to-do item makes it more difficult for you to give up on it

- Setting goals
- Telling the world about your plans through social media—peer pressure is powerful

Finally, a word of caution: There are times when we should simply throw in the towel and give up on a project or goal. Remember that old saying, "If your horse is dead, get off and start walking"? This metaphor applies to many facets of our lives—don't try to ride a dead horse.

Productivity Boosters and Productivity Compounding

We have all experienced situations where we are far more productive or, unfortunately, far less productive than we would like to be. Often this is a function of either the enjoyment that we get from the task at hand or the urgency of the situation. If we don't enjoy a task and it is not urgent, we tend to procrastinate. Let's look at a couple of examples to illustrate this point.

I exercise regularly and really enjoy being active. However, I really don't like swimming for any time period longer than a few minutes. Bike riding, on the other hand, I will do for hours. The length of the exercise program is simply a function of what I enjoy. The lesson here is to be aware of what works for you and what does not.

Similarly, the urgency of the situation improves productivity. For example, think back to a project at work that had an impossible deadline and yet you got it done. You couldn't work at that pace everyday, but in the short term, your productivity improved dramatically.

Now, let's talk about productivity compounding. Productivity, like your finances, can be compounded. If you set a goal of becoming 10% more productive each year for seven years, at the end of the seven years, through the magic of compounding, you will be approximately 100% more productive. Keep in mind that almost everyone can improve their productivity by 10% a year using some of the tips in this chapter.

6. Productivity

Avoid Just Being Busy—Busy Work Is a Productivity Killer

Keep in mind that most busy work tends to focus on mindless tasks that you could almost do in your sleep. By its very nature, it's repetitive and easy to do and may have to be done but not necessarily by you, or perhaps not in the time-consuming manner that you are currently doing it.

Here are a few suggestions that may help you get rid of some of the busy work that is currently consuming far too much of your time:

- Take a few minutes during the day to record each task that you do in a journal. At the end of the week (or month, if that is more appropriate), review the task journal and decide which task to drop or delegate and resolve to never do these tasks again.
- Again, using your task journal, review the tasks that should be a higher priority and resolve to give them the time and priority that they deserve.
- Commit to shorter communications. Remember, that no one really wants to read a three-page email from you, brilliant as it may be. As Einstein said, if you can't explain something simply, you don't understand it well enough, and simple generally means keeping it short and to the point.
- Plan your day and set priorities. This sounds like a no-brainer, but prioritizing your activities will make you far more productive.
- Remember, getting started on a task is often the hardest step. If you are stuck in neutral, go for a short walk. Exercise often generates ideas seemingly out of nowhere.
- Use the one-touch system for those tasks that come up during the day but are not on your to-do list. This system is great for immediate priorities, especially if you can delegate them. Some tasks should be put on your to-do list to be handled later, but many can be done immediately using the one-touch system.

- If, despite your best efforts, you still have busy work that you cannot drop or delegate, do them all together during your least productive time of day.

Avoid Multi-Tasking

I'm a big believer in the power of focusing on one activity at a time. No one can realistically do more than one complex task at one time, and when you multi-task, you become less productive because you lose time figuring out where you were in the last project before you jumped to a new one.

Most of us can walk and chew gum at the same time, but jumping from one complex goal to another is beyond us. Focus on your top priority first and then move on to the next priority.

Limit Social Media

Social media, as we all know, can be huge time waster and a productivity killer. Only you will know if this is a problem for you.

Summary

In closing, I'd like to leave you with a few productivity tips that work for me. There is no magic productivity formula, but give these ideas a try:

- *Peer pressure:* If you tell your spouse and friends, or better yet, post your goals on social media, you will definitely feel the pressure to achieve them. No one likes to have the world think that they have failed, so ensure that you are committed before you take this step. Peer pressure will make you more productive, but it will also increase your stress level.
- *Exercise:* If I am stuck and can't seem to move forward, I have found that going for a walk or a bike ride often helps

6. Productivity

productivity. Taking a break to become more productive seems counterintuitive, but it works.

- *Brainstorming:* Spend half an hour with a trusted advisor, or even by yourself, and document your thoughts on a white board or on your computer. Just the act of putting your thoughts to writing will often help you generate new ideas and become more productive.

Set interim targets with deadlines: For example, if your ultimate goal is to lose twenty pounds, set monthly goals of two pounds a month. This will help keep you motivated and more productive.

- *Push yourself:* Think back to your high school gym classes and that gym teacher who was trying to get you into shape. Remember how he kept asking for just two more sit-ups? You can use this technique to become more productive by forcing yourself, for example, to make five more cold calls a day or write two more pages in a proposal before you go home.

- *Think about your options:* In keeping with the theme of this book—that life really isn't that complicated, but you do have to think—you will often dramatically improve your productivity by simply listing all the options that you have to resolve a particular problem. For example, if you know that your checking account is going to be overdrawn this month, you have several options to proactively resolve this problem:
  - Do nothing and hope that your financial institution won't bounce your cheques.
  - Take out a loan to cover the overdraft.
  - Talk to your financial institution about the expense involved with having overdraft protection on your account.
  - Charge everything to your credit card(s) this month rather than write cheques that might bounce.
  - Don't pay a few of your bills this month so your account isn't overdrawn.

What you decide to do depends on your personal financial situation. The point is that you have options to think about, and when you are reviewing your options, remember Occam's razor and think horses, not zebras.

Remember, productivity can be learned and is simply a by-product of good habits, conscious decisions, and careful thought; keep in mind that productive people are not just busy, they produce something useful.

📝 Your homework is to resolve to use one productivity tip from this book each week for a period of at least eight weeks. At the end of the eight weeks, critically analyze your productivity improvement.

Finally, a few quotes that may inspire you:

"Patience, persistence and perspiration make an unbelievable combination for success."
— NAPOLEON HILL

"The Principle of Priority states (a) you must know the difference between what is urgent and what is important, and (b) you must do what is important first."
— STEVEN PRESSFIELD

"Focus on being productive instead of busy."
— TIM FERRISS

7. Religion and Moral Code

"My religion is very simple. My religion is kindness."
— DALAI LAMA, XIV

What Is Your Moral Code?

I have been extremely confused about religion almost my entire life. I was baptized and confirmed in the Catholic Church, but from my early teens, I struggled with my faith. I think back now to my childhood and going to Catholic religious services in the 1950s—which were primarily in Latin, with a priest in robes, incense, and chanting—and confessing to a priest, on a weekly basis, of all my sins. I was just a kid trying to get by in what was already a very confusing world. Latin services followed by a very stressful confession, which were followed by many Hail Marys as penance, didn't really help me become a better person.

Two other issues in my formative years compounded my personal confusion about religion. First, religion was a source of a great deal of stress in my parents' marriage. My father was raised as a Lutheran, while my mother was Catholic. For them to marry, my father had to convert to the Catholic faith and agree to raise their children as Catholics. This caused major issues between my parents, which us children witnessed. Second, in my teenage years, two of my friends died in tragic car accidents. As a teenager, I was deeply troubled by their deaths. We all want to believe that there is life after death, but

I couldn't understand the deaths of two young men and the grief it caused their friends and family.

Perhaps now that you know a little of my background, you will understand why I have always found organized religion to be deeply troubling.

George Carlin said it best for me:

> *"Religion has actually convinced people that there is an invisible man, living in the sky, who watches everything that you do every day of your life. And he has a list of ten things that he does not want you to do. And if you do any, any, of these ten things he has a special place full of fire and smoke and ash and torture where he will send you to suffer and burn and scream and cry forever and ever until the end of time!*
>
> *But He loves you. He loves you, and He needs money!"*

If your faith is strong and you are living your life tied to religious beliefs that are guiding you in keeping with your religious doctrine, then skip this chapter.

If you are struggling with your faith and the moral direction of your life, as I am, then I suggest that you develop your own personal moral code and commit to living your life in alignment with this code. This is not nearly as difficult as it sounds, but you will have to think and commit to an action plan. You don't have to swear to perfection, but you do have to think about your moral code and swear on a stack of Darwin's *The Origins of Species* that you will try to evolve to a better state of being.

Let's start with a few issues with Christianity that I have problem with.

Biblical Stories Are Troubling

The Bible includes several stories that are difficult to believe, but before I begin to look at Biblical stories that stretch the limits of credibility, I would like to relate a story about one of my grandsons and his view on the Christmas elf that many parents move around the house before Christmas. For those of you not familiar with the Christmas elf, parents put the elf up in various places around the house and tell the children that the elf reports back to Santa every night about their behaviour. When my son was explaining this to my three-year-old grandson, he looked at my son, his father, with a very jaundiced eye, shook his head, and walked away mumbling that he couldn't see how the elf could fly to the North Pole and back every night.

I can see that some of you are shaking your head and wondering what this story, cute as it may be, has to do with the Christian religion. The point is that a three-year-old could see through the Christmas elf fantasy, but we, for centuries, have accepted as gospel the many fairy tales in the Bible. I have outlined a few of them below.

The Virgin Birth

Mary, the mother of Jesus, was by all Biblical accounts a virgin when she gave birth to Jesus, the son of God. It just wouldn't do for the mother of the son of God to be tainted by sex. Really?

Noah and the Ark

The story of Noah building an ark to house his family and two of all the creatures of the earth to save them from a flood is very well known. It can be found in the Old Testament and the Koran. Think about this. First, God plans to drown all the other animals and all people other than Noah and his family. Sounds quite nasty to me. Second, can you imagine a wooden boat with two of every creature on earth in it? Even my three-year-old grandson could see through this story as well.

Jonah and the Whale

In this story, Jonah was apparently swallowed by a whale who then spit him out unharmed. Again, I say, really?

You shouldn't have to turn your brain off in order to be a good Christian.

Common Religious Expressions that Trouble Me

Here are a few religious expressions that are commonly used that blow my mind:

- *"God has a plan for you":* There are approximately eight billion people on earth, and God is planning all our lives? Should we really be sitting back and waiting for the plan to unfold for us?
- *"God works in strange and mysterious ways":* This is just a cop-out. This expression was commonly used around the time of the deaths of two of my teenage friends.
- *"God won't give you more than you can handle":* Can the children of Africa handle starvation?
- *"God will provide"* and contrast that with *"The Lord helps those who help themselves."*

The Story of Creation Is Also Deeply Troubling

When I imagine God creating the earth and all the creatures on it, the first thing that comes to mind is that for an omnipotent entity he/she really didn't think this through. In order to survive, the majority of the earth's creatures eat each other. We, for the most part, are at the top of the food chain, but it hasn't always been that way. Anthropologists have discovered caves full of human bones with unmistakable evidence of animal teeth marks. We were the hunted as well as the hunters. Survival of the fittest rolls off the tongue very easily, but picture yourself on the "being eaten" end of the equation!

I will leave you with this thought: if you were an omnipotent god, would you design a universe in which the creatures in your creation ate each other to survive?

Cafeteria Christians

Cafeteria Christianity or "Christianity Lite" is a term used to describe Christians who pick and choose the Christian doctrines that suit them and reject those that don't. Typically, this involves Christian doctrines such as homosexuality, abortion, premarital sex, and capital punishment.

The Bible is very clear on these topics. Take homosexuality for example. Death is required for homosexuals, so clearly the Bible has no issue with capital punishment either.

Can you really be a good Christian while picking those Christian doctrines that suit you and rejecting those you don't?

Other Humans in the Homo Genus

According to Christian teachings, we were created in God's image. However, archeologists have discovered evidence of many other human families in addition to Homo sapiens (the name given by anthropologists to all humans alive today). These include the following, in no particular order:

- Neanderthals
- Denisovans
- Homo erectus
- Homo habilis
- Homo rudolfensis
- numerous others

In fact, most of today's humans of European descent have approximately 2% of the Neanderthal genome.

This gets us into the whole "creation versus evolution" debate, and I really don't want to go there, but it raises the question, which branch of the human tree was created in God's image?

Thousands of Gods

Out of curiosity, I did a search to get an estimate on the number of gods that humans have worshipped over the millennia. Eight thousand to twelve thousand was the estimate. This too is clearly troubling, even if the estimate is out by a factor of ten.

What are the odds that our Christian God is the correct one?

My Personal Moral Code

Enough about religion and what I don't believe in. I have struggled with my faith, but I do have a personal moral code that I try to live by. Like you, I've made mistakes and have had to step back to re-evaluate how I am living my life. This book has helped me to do just that, as it forces clarity of thought if you must write it for others to analyze. Moral perfection has certainly eluded me, but I like to think that I am at least moving in the right direction.

I hope that I don't sound "holier than thou," but I've outlined a summary of my moral code below:

- Treat others as you want to be treated. This of course is just the Golden Rule that we were all taught by our parents. It's a very simple, and perhaps trite, but powerful principle that we have all violated. Following the Golden Rule eliminates a multitude of sins.

- Accept responsibility for your thoughts and actions with few, if any, exceptions. Personal responsibility requires us to "man or woman up" and accept responsibility for our screw ups. Blaming your mother is not allowed.

- The rule of law applies to all of us. Laws are in place to protect us from ourselves. If you believe that a law is morally wrong, work to change it. Keep in mind that the rule of law trumps freedom of speech and freedom of religion, as there are hundreds, if not thousands, of religious sects.

7. Religion and Moral Code

- Freedom of religion is mandatory in any civilized society. Respect other's religious rights. We are all free to worship as we see fit, within the rule of law. In other words, you cannot, for example, practise a religion that allows the male church elders to marry underage girls. Sound familiar?
- Freedom of speech is also a fundamental tenet of democracy. We all have a right to freely speak as we believe. Political correctness should not be used to muzzle dissenting opinions. This is a grave danger to our democratic way of life. A caveat to this is freedom of the press. Non-democratic societies tend to violate this principle.
- Forgive and forget transgressions of the past. This applies to yourself and others.
- And finally, don't steal, don't cheat, and don't lie. This is just Morality 101.

The Ten Commandments—A Christian Moral Code?

If you think about it, Christianity outlines a simple moral code for us—the Ten Commandments:

1. You shall have no other gods before me.
2. You shall not make for yourself an idol.
3. You shall not misuse the name of the Lord your God.
4. Remember the Sabbath day by keeping it holy.
5. Honour your father and mother.
6. You shall not murder.
7. You shall not commit adultery.
8. You shall not steal.
9. You shall not give false testimony against your neighbour.
10. You shall not covet.

As you might suspect, I have few problems with the Ten Commandments. Rules one through four relate to worship of this supreme being, but I can accept rules five to ten as valid. However, having the first four commandments focused on worshiping a supreme being seems to me to be overkill. Surely, one rule on worshipping the supreme being and nine on how to live a better life would be a more appropriate balance. Love thy neighbour as thyself might be a useful addition.

Shouldn't the goal of religion be to help us become better people?

Summary

I have spent a great deal of time agonizing over this chapter on religion, and despite my best efforts, I feel that I have let you the reader down. Religion is a very complex subject, and I only touched briefly on one religion, Christianity. Religious beliefs are very personal and become an essential part of who we are.

In this chapter, I have only touched the highlights of the problems with one religion, and there have been hundreds, if not thousands, of religious sects practised by humans throughout history. All have their issues, but humans do seem to need a moral compass with some kind of divine focus to lead us to a better way.

So, as an alternative to a formal religion, what do I recommend?

First, I suggest that we all think about and decide to live by a personal moral code. I have outlined my personal moral code earlier in this chapter.

Second, find a good charity to support. Many in this world need our help. As a society, we have an obligation to offer a helping hand. For those of you who financially support a church, I suggest that you take some (all?) of that money and contribute it to a good charity. The world will be a better place for it.

I hope that this chapter has, at the very least, made you think about your religious beliefs but, more importantly, about how you are going to change your life. Again, I hate to sound holier than thou, but we can all work to make this world a better place. Remember, goals without

7. Religion and Moral Code

actions are just dreams, so when I say "work to make this world a better place," I really mean that work is required.

- 📝 With that in mind, your homework is to sit down for an hour or two and document your personal moral code that you are committed to. The words to "Imagine," written by John Lennon of the Beatles, were an inspiration to me. They may be to you as well. Do a quick search online for the words as additional homework.

8. Time Management

"The way we spend our time defines who we are."
— JONATHON ESTRIN

How Can You Successfully Manage Your Time?

Let's be honest, time can't really be managed in any meaningful way as, for example, money can be managed. We can earn more or less money and spend more or less money, but despite our best efforts, time marches relentlessly on and refuses to be managed. Without getting philosophical about time, keep in mind that even if you live to be a 100 years old, you will only have approximately 5,200 weeks in your life and we all have 24 hours a day and 600 minutes in even a 10-hour workday. We can't change any of this.

All we can really do is take steps to ensure that we spend the time that we have productively while still leaving time for the people we love and the activities that we truly enjoy. Consider this my very simple definition of time management.

For the remainder of this chapter, I will outline the steps that I learned to ensure that I spend my time at least reasonably productively.

8. Time Management

Do It, Delegate It, or Drop It

"Do it, delegate it, or drop it" was a mantra that I used very often during my working career. Now that I am retired, I really don't have anyone to delegate to, so "delegate it" really means hire someone to do the job for me.

Very often the "do it" part of the mantra is easily handled by taking the first few steps. Starting is key, and once you start, the next steps follow naturally. If you can't see your way clearly to the first few actions, then you may need to research the project more or consider getting help.

Projects that just hang around, seemingly forever, are stress creators—they are always in the back of my mind keeping me awake at night—so if the project is not in my area of expertise, I either hire someone to do it or, if possible, drop the project entirely. Try this system and you will sleep better.

Get Your Priorities In Order

I have already spent a some time on priorities in chapters 2 and 6, so I am not going to repeat it all here, but getting your priorities in the correct order will greatly simplify your life and save you time and money. For most people, this doesn't involve anything more than thinking things through and following up appropriately. Don't focus on the trivial at the expense of the important. A classic example of the trivial getting more time than the important is the fact that many people spend as much time buying new clothes as they spend on a vehicle purchase, despite the fact the latter costs many time more than the former and has a far greater impact on their life.

Just Get Started

The best advice that I can give anyone once they have determined their priorities is to just get started. The first step is always the most difficult, but once you have taken the first step, the next steps will follow. It's the old story about the journey of a thousand miles beginning with the first step.

For example, when I was thinking about writing this book, I read a few books about writing a book and, of course, have read hundreds of books in a lifetime of learning. One book on how to write a book stated quite clearly that if you want to write a book, you should just start writing. I took this advice to heart and wrote an outline for each of the chapters and then followed up by writing the first chapter. The process wasn't linear by any means, but once I started, I saved a great deal of time by not spinning my wheels and overthinking the book-writing process. I concluded that if I want to be a writer, I should begin by writing.

Use Technology

We live in an age of amazing technology that can save you a great deal of time. Just think of the tools that you have available to you:

- search engines that provide you with access to information on any topic;
- social media;
- email and instant messaging to contact experts;
- productivity tools such as spreadsheets and word processing;
- financial analysis tools;
- artificial intelligence;
- online books and book summaries on any topic;
- video conferencing;
- team management tools;
- SMART objectives and action plans for many projects; and,
- the list goes on and on.

I don't start any project without using technology to research the topic. For example, a few years ago, I had to cut down a tree. I had a small chainsaw and knew how to use it but didn't know how to get the tree to fall exactly where I wanted it to fall. After a few minutes online, I had the answer. This is a trivial example, but you get the idea—use technology to save you time.

Keep in mind that these tools can be a great time waster as well. Social networking is a classic example.

Use the 80/20 Principle (Pareto Principle)

As I have outlined earlier, the 80/20 Principle states that 80% of results very often comes from 20% of your inputs. In other words, 20% of your work produces 80% of the benefit. Clearly the numbers are not absolutes. In some cases, the ratio is 90/10 or 60/40. The point is that very often the results are disproportionate to the effort expended. The classic example for companies is that often 20% of their customers produce 80% of their revenue and often more than 80% of their profit.

This principle can be a great time saver for individuals as well, if we give the application of the principle some thought. For example:

When studying for an exam, you are very likely to get a better return for the time you invest by reviewing your lecture notes than trying to read through the entire text book.

When reviewing your investment returns, focus on the top 20% in terms of amount invested first and later, time permitting, the bottom 80%.

Use Occam's Razor

Occam's razor, as I've already explained, is a heuristic, or rule of thumb, that states that whenever you are faced with multiple explanations for a problem or situation, the simplest one is most likely the correct one.

If the simplest explanation is usually the correct one, we can use this principle to become more productive and save time. Remember the metaphor, if you hear hoof beats, think horses, not zebras.

Motivate Yourself—Keep Track of Your Progress and Reward Yourself

If all you do each day is grind through your to-do list and check off your action plans to reach your goals, you will find that you soon burn out. We all need the motivation of rewards to keep us going. This may be as small and simple as a coffee break after a long conference call or as large as a vacation at the end of a major successful project. We all need rewards and fun to keep us motivated.

Become an Early Riser

I was an early riser during my working career, and I found that an hour in the morning was worth two afternoon hours. My last career step involved working with staff from around the world in many time zones. Because of this, I typically started my day with my first coffee at 5:00 a.m., had a quick fifteen-minute breakfast break around 9:00, and lunch followed by a nap around 2:00. Most days, I exercised for an hour about 4:00 and worked again from 5:00 to 6:00 p.m.

This worked for me because of the time zone issue and because I was far more productive in the early morning. However, as I outlined earlier, when it comes to exercise, I am not an early morning person.

If you research the topic of early risers, you will find that many of the world's most successful people are very early risers. Check it out.

Exercise

I used to be a jogger, but now that my knees can't handle jogging any more, I ride a bike to get my exercise "fix" and I have found that many of my best time-saving ideas come, seemingly out of the blue, when I am exercising.

This is not a phenomenon that I have researched, but it most definitely works for me. Give it a try, and if nothing else, you will be healthier as a result of the exercise.

Try Parkinson's Law

Parkinson's Law, that we are all familiar with, states that work expands to fill the time allotted. We have all seen this law in action. For example, in any work-related task, if we know the deadline is at the end of the week, its amazing how often we are crossing the t's and dotting the i's at the last minute. However, if the same task had an end-of-day deadline, its equally amazing how we still managed to get the job done.

You can use Parkinson's Law to save time by setting a somewhat arbitrary shortened deadline for a task. Try it, it works.

Consider Parkinson's Law of Triviality

Parkinson's Law of Triviality is based on the observation that most of us spend a disproportionate amount of time on the trivial while neglecting the critical. We do this because often, the trivial tasks are easy while the important tasks are far more difficult. Human nature results in us taking the easy path.

For example, if you decide to do a financial review to determine how you save more for your retirement, think about how you can make your car last a few more years and not how you can save a few cents on gas by going to a different gas station.

Think about your personal situation and how you can use this principle to save time.

Plan for Murphy's Law

Murphy's law in states that if something can go wrong, it very likely will. A little thought can very often save you a great deal of time by averting a disaster. For example, if you have a proposal to deliver to a client, how often has your printer run out of ink and you don't have any extra cartridges, or you are required to research a topic and your Wi-Fi is down?

The point is that we all need to plan for critical projects and their possible pit falls. Issues may arise that you did not anticipate, but at least plan for the obvious ones.

Take Ownership

Taking ownership of your time is the last major point that we need to review. You are responsible for how you spend your time. Your manager or your spouse can't look over you shoulder 24/7. You must decide on the priorities in your life. Don't waste your life on the trivial.

Miscellaneous Time Management Thoughts

Procrastination and unfinished tasks cause stress and slow you down by renting space in your head. Many tasks can be done in a few minutes if you just get started. Try the following miscellaneous time management tools:

- *One-touch system:* Small tasks can often be done in one iteration as you think of them.
- *Preplan your day:* Take ten minutes to lay out a rough draft of your time in time blocks.
- *Avoid meetings:* Most meetings are a huge time waster.
- *Handle emails only once or twice each day:* This is self explanatory.
- *Use to-do lists:* Don't rely on your memory.
- *Set somewhat artificial deadlines:* If a task usually takes two hours, try a deadline of one hour.
- *Use sub-tasks:* Almost all projects have milestones; use the milestones in combination with artificial deadlines.

8. Time Management

Compounding Time Management

If you set a goal for yourself of becoming 6% better at time management each week, for twelve weeks, using the techniques discussed in this book, at the end of only twelve weeks, you will have improved 100%. Compounding works for many aspects of our life, not just finance.

📝 Your homework is to follow the twelve-week program outlined below:

- **Week One:** Commit to using a to-do list every day. This can be on your laptop, phone, or even paper. Challenge yourself, but don't set completely unrealistic lists.
- **Week Two:** Fine tune your to-do list by using the 80/20 Principle and putting the most important tasks first on your list to ensure that they are complete by day's end.
- **Week Three:** Resolve to use the one-touch system for smaller tasks.
- **Week Four:** Set somewhat artificially short deadlines for tasks and sub-tasks on your to-do list and resolve to meet these deadlines.
- **Week Five:** Handle emails only twice a day—once in the morning and once at the end of your work day. Don't spend more than half an hour each time.
- **Week Six:** Establish an early morning routine that requires you to get up an hour early and exercise for a minimum of forty-five minutes followed by a shower.
- **Week Seven:** Eliminate at least two trivial recurring tasks.
- **Week Eight:** Review your to-do lists for the first seven weeks and decide to continue to do them, delegate them, or drop them. Be ruthless.
- **Week Nine:** Review your to-do lists again and spend at least an hour thinking about how technology could help you save time in the future and resolve to make the appropriate changes.

- **Week Ten:** Limit social media to two hours a week.
- **Week Eleven:** Review your progress with a mentor or close work friend and listen carefully to their input with a view to further improvement.
- **Week Twelve:** Reward yourself with an evening out with your significant other or close friend. We all deserve rewards and rewards can be a great source of motivation.

Clearly, there is no magic in twelve weeks other than that twelve goes evenly in seventy-two, so your time management skills increase by 100% (the Rule of 72 is explained in the Chapter 4). Also, keep in mind that in some weeks, your time management will improve much more than 6%.

Of course, it goes without saying that for compound growth to occur, the week-one activity must continue to week two, the week-two activity continue to week three, and so on. Each step builds on the previous.

9. Play It Again Sam

I'm not going to repeat all the points that I've covered in this book, but I am going to highlight a few in this "Play It Again Sam" chapter. I'm arrogant enough to think that all the chapters are important, but for this summary, I'm only going to cover the following six chapters, and I'm going to leave you with what I consider to be the keys to a very happy and successful life.

1. *Find your genius:* Sam's genius was his people skills.
2. *Health and wellness:* Without your health, nothing else matters.
3. *Habits:* If you find your genius and have good habits, you will be successful.
4. *Goals:* Every goal has a price. Are you willing to pay the price?
5. Finance: Money isn't everything, but it does make life easier.
6. *Religion and moral code:* Decide what your moral code is and live it.

Find Your Genius—People Skills May Be the Answer

Almost every profession requires good interpersonal skills. Think of the most successful people you know:
- your favourite teacher
- the hardware store you always return to because of the owner
- the boss who you would always go the extra mile for

- the real estate agent who has countless repeat clients
- your doctor who always had time to explain your medical problem in layman terms

You get the message. Successful people have excellent people skills. I've outlined a few key skills below.

Like, Trust, and Respect

You may have heard this a hundred times, but it is worth repeating: if people like you, trust you, and respect you, they will work with you. These three attributes are key to your success.

Sam, the free-range chicken, had excellent people skills, even as a teenager, and was always willing to work with those he liked, trusted, and respected. This was evident in a story Sam related to me many years ago about an interaction he had with my father, the principal of the high school. When Sam was a senior in high school, he decided to grow a beard, and my father, being very conservative, decided that it just wouldn't do for high school students to have beards. My father called Sam into his office and proceeded to try to talk him into shaving. Dad appealed to Sam's vanity by suggesting that as one of the school's leaders, he would appreciate it if Sam shaved off the beard so that the other boys, the followers, didn't grow one as well. Sam understood exactly what my father was doing in appealing to his vanity by suggesting that he was a school leader, but Sam liked, trusted, and respected my father. He knew that my father didn't have a leg to stand on in terms of school policy and beards, but the next day, the beard was gone.

This simple interaction between a student and the principal clearly illustrates how valuable it can be to have people like, trust, and respect you. Everything being equal, and often when it is not equal, people gravitate to working with those they like, trust, and respect. I have seen this countless times with my wife, who is an excellent judge of character. If my wife perceives that a salesperson, for example, lacks one or more of these traits, she will not work with them. However, if she is doing business with someone she does like, trust, and respect, she will go the extra mile for them even in the face of problems.

Communication Skill

Successful people communicate their ideas clearly, simply, and in terms the audience understands. As I said earlier, Einstein believed that if you can't explain something in simple terms, you don't understand it well enough.

During my career, I sat through countless technical IT presentations. Some presenters went to great pains to present in a clear and straight forward manner. Others were very difficult to follow and seemed more intent on impressing the audience than they were on communicating a key message.

Listening Skill

If you listen carefully, people will tell you what you need to know, but they often will hide it in a great deal of dialogue and you will have to pay close attention to what they are saying and, of course, you may also have to read between the lines. This is true in almost all interpersonal interactions, including sales, hiring, management, and the list goes on. Just listen and reiterate the key points that the speaker is making so that the he knows that you clearly understood. Don't be thinking about what you are going to say next while the speaker is speaking. As a corollary to listening carefully, ensure that you don't sell past the close. Once the other side has stated agreement with you, close the deal. This applies to true "sales" situations and any interaction in which you require agreement.

Empathy

This is a characteristic that you can't "fake it until you make it." People intuitively know when someone truly feels their pain and when they don't. Look people in the eye, listen carefully, and offer help where you can.

Health and Wellness

The health and wellness chapter should resonate with everyone, as we have all had at least a minor health issue. After years of researching and experimenting with what works for me, I found that if I was struggling mentally or physically, I could narrow it down to a problem with one or more of the following seven key areas:

1. *Nutrition:* Follow the Canada food guide.
2. *Exercise:* Start with half an hour a day of walking, swimming, or biking.
3. *Sleep and rest:* Eight hours sleep works for most people.
4. *Social interaction:* Even lone wolves need people in their life.
5. *Mental health:* Find a trusted person to confide in.
6. *Sense of purpose:* Find something to look forward to and don't let fear of failure stop you from a new project.
7. *Balance:* Set your priorities and live your life in alignment with them.

Pay attention to these seven key ingredients to health and wellness and your mental and physical health will improve.

Successful Habits

If you find your genius and have successful habits, I can almost guarantee that you will have a very successful and fulfilling life. Change your habits, change your life.

You can't control your genetic makeup and you often have limited control of your environment, but you can change your habits. Start with the areas of your life that provide the greatest impact:

- *Your health:* Start by walking half an hour a day and eating healthy.

9. Play It Again Sam

- *Your finances:* Live slightly below your means and save the difference.
- *Eliminate one bad habit:* Only you know what this is.

Goals

In order to achieve your goals, you must be willing to pay the price. Goals and action plans go hand-in-hand—no exceptions.

For example, if you want to lose twenty pounds, an action plan involving diet and exercise is required. You must be willing to pay the price required to achieve your goal; otherwise, you are just kidding yourself.

Finance

The slow-and-steady investment growth system outlined in the finance chapter requires you to first take positive steps to improve your income and then analyze your expenses to:

- determine how much discretionary income you have each month;
- save a set percentage of your discretionary income in a pension fund, TFSA, RRSP, or all three—in other words, pay yourself first; and,
- watch your investments grow tax free with time and the magic of compound interest—remember, investing is a marathon not a sprint.

This system works, as the following example of the power of compound interest illustrates:

- Initial age that you begin investing: 40
- Principal amount when you begin investing at age 40: $0
- Monthly saving amount: $500
- Rate of return: 7%

- Value of your investment at age 65: $393,735

You invested $150,000 (twenty-five years multiplied by twelve months per year multiplied by $500 per month) and the money grew to $393,735 with the magic of compound interest.

Religion and Moral Code

Religious beliefs are very personal and often go to a person's core values. We all have to recognize that everyone has a right to worship as they see fit. The corollary is that the rule of law trumps all religious beliefs since, as we all know, there have been religions in the past that had practices we find repugnant today.

Religion can also be very complex and confusing, but as a first step, I suggest that if you believe in a supreme being that created the heavens and the earth, do some research and pick a religion that aligns with *your* beliefs and values. There are many religions to pick from.

If you don't believe in a supreme being, decide on a personal moral code and live your life in alignment with your moral code.

Religion doesn't need to be nearly as complicated as we make it.

Personal Responsibility

My almost last message to you is to accept personal responsibility for how you live your life. We are all individually responsible for our thoughts, words and actions. For most of us, blaming your mother or father is not allowed past the age of six.

You are responsible!

Keys to a Happy and Successful Life—It all Boils Down to This!

First and foremost, find and keep a partner you love and who loves you. I am not qualified to write on this topic, but it is imperative that you get it correct. There is a great deal of information available, so do

9. Play It Again Sam

the research. I got lucky and married an amazing woman, but this really was serendipity.

Once you have found a loving life partner, focus on:

- finding your genius—we all have at least one;
- developing good habits, particularly in the areas of health and finance; and,
- setting goals and relentlessly pursuing them with action plans.

I can almost hear some of you thinking, "It took a whole book to make these points!"

CPSIA information can be obtained
at www.ICGtesting.com
Printed in the USA
JSHW022100150723
44289JS00009B/171/J